D0977335

HERO DOGS

HERO DOGS

How a Pack of Rescues, Rejects,
and Strays Became America's
Greatest Disaster-Search Partners

Wilma Melville with Paul Lobo

St. Martin's Press ≋ New York

HERO DOGS. Copyright © 2019 by Wilma
Melville with Paul Lobo. All rights reserved.
Printed in the United States of America. For
information, address St. Martin's Press, 175
Fifth Avenue, New York, N.Y. 10010.

www.stmartins.com

The Library of Congress Cataloging-in-
Publication Data is available upon request.

ISBN 978-1-250-17991-3 (hardcover)
ISBN 978-1-250-17992-0 (ebook)

Our books may be purchased in bulk
for promotional, educational, or business
use. Please contact your local bookseller
or the Macmillan Corporate and
Premium Sales Department at 1-800-
221-7945, extension 5442, or by email at
MacmillanSpecialMarkets@macmillan.com.

First Edition: January 2019

10 9 8 7 6 5 4 3 2 1

For the whole pack

Until one is committed, there is hesitancy, the chance to draw back, always ineffectiveness. Concerning all acts of initiative and creation, there is one elementary truth the ignorance of which kills countless ideas and splendid plans: that the moment one definitely commits oneself, then providence moves too.

—JOHANN WOLFGANG VON GOETHE

PART I

Let's go search! *Paul Lobo*

One

WATCH HER GO

I knew we were in for a show the instant I dropped the leash.

Murphy was off so fast her paws barely touched the ground. Only sixteen weeks old, the Black Labrador was nowhere near her adult size, but her hips and chest were thick with corded muscle and every ounce of her body—every fiber it seemed—was engaged in the run. She blasted across the training area near Bakersfield, her legs a blur, kicking up rooster tails of red California dirt. A few yards in front of her, and growing ever closer, was an odd conglomerate of large blue plastic tubes, lined up in a row like someone had laid down a giant pan flute on its side. The tubes were as wide as large oil drums and stretched over ten feet long. Somewhere in those tubes was a person in need of rescue.

It was 1993 and I'd been training to become a canine search-and-rescue (SAR) handler for a few years. I'd done my part. Now the determination of who would be my partner was up to Murphy.

She suddenly cut right so fast her tongue maintained its former trajectory and flapped out to the side like a pink flag. As she flew past the first couple sealed tubes, I felt my stomach knot in doubt. Perhaps I'd been overconfident coming into the session. Perhaps she wasn't ready for this level of search yet.

Murphy had been seven weeks old when I'd purchased her from a family who professionally bred hunting dogs. The transaction had been quick—just long enough for the breeders to give advice on feeding patterns—then the tiny pompom of a pup had been placed in my arms like a furry receipt. Silent and docile, she'd slept all the way home. I was a little worried. Search dogs need to be bursting with energy. Cute as she was, I couldn't help but wonder if I'd purchased a dud search dog. I didn't wonder long.

I mixed her a bowl of the prescribed food while she sat uninterested in the corner. Without much thought, I lowered the bowl toward the kitchen floor.

Murphy exploded out of the corner like a rocket. This dark projectile launched toward me and punched the food bowl out of my hands. The kibble sprayed into the air and rained down onto the kitchen tile. I was frozen in disbelief.

Murphy was not. She morphed from rocket into vacuum cleaner and sucked down every morsel of food within minutes, leaving the kitchen tile looking as if nothing had ever happened. Murphy licked her chops and, with a yawn, retired behind her indifferent puppy façade. My shock gave way to glee. It looked like I might have a search dog on my hands after all.

Nine weeks later I was watching Murphy zip across our volunteer group's SAR proving grounds. A number of Swiss disaster search dog trainers had flown in to teach advanced canine search techniques and evaluate some of our up-and-coming dogs. When it came to canine search, the Swiss were the gold standard. They pioneered canine search around 1800, patrolling the Great St. Bernard Pass and other high peaks in Switzerland for lost outdoorsmen. If Murphy truly had what it took to be a search dog, the Swiss trainers would know.

Now, one of the trainers waited, hidden in a blue tube, as Murphy closed in. My dog would need to complete two tasks. First, locate the tube where the trainer was hiding and give a bark alert—bark consistently at the hidden human until that person was revealed. After she succeeded in locating the "victim," Murphy would still need to show a continued drive—what we call "prey drive"—until she got her reward. In her case, the reward, or "prey," being a worn-out chew toy. These tasks would show not only that Murphy could use her nose to find a buried human, but also be motivated to continue searching after the initial victim was found. Both tasks would need passing grades if I wanted to consider her for serious search dog training. There was no middle ground.

Murphy zeroed in on the middle tube and stopped dead. Her tail started lashing back and forth and she launched into a chorus of barks. I heard the muffled praise from the hidden trainer. Murphy kept up her consistent bark alert. So far, she was performing a textbook search. One box checked, one to go.

The lid of the blue tube popped open. We'd now see if Murphy's drive would hold strong until she received her reward. Time seemed to pause as the trainer began to squirm out of the tube.

Then Murphy charged forward. The trainer's feet hadn't even cleared the lid as Murphy plowed over him and into the tube, searching for the chew toy he was hiding. I heard the delighted hooting of the trainer as he wrestled and teased Murphy with the toy, making her work just a little more. Then both emerged, the trainer smiling broadly and Murphy strutting triumphantly with the toy dangling from her mouth. It was beautiful.

"You can make *many* mistakes with this one," the trainer said with a thick German accent, patting Murphy's head.

He meant the dog had such a strong prey drive, the handler wouldn't need to do much except get out of the way. In search dog parlance, he'd just given Murphy the equivalent of an A+. She still had a long way to go before she was deployment ready, but there was now no doubt in my mind Murphy was a special dog.

What I didn't know was that, for what was looming over the horizon, she would have to be.

Two

FROM THE SHADOW OF EVIL: OKLAHOMA CITY, OK

didn't know why the line wasn't moving. I craned my neck over the firefighter in front of me, trying to identify the holdup. The long column of search dog handlers and rescue workers stretching down the bus's main aisle would move forward a few steps then stop abruptly, causing a bumper-car effect for everyone still confined on the bus. Step. Stop. Bump. Repeat. What on earth was going on?

I dislike inaction in any form. That was part of the reason after I'd retired from teaching I'd wanted to become a search dog handler. But a disdain for inaction was only part of the equation.

I've been known to push limits. Have my entire life.

Initiative and persistence—the broken-down-then-rebuilt-until-strong kind of persistence—are an integral part of my personal philosophy. I'm not a hard case; I just feel the world is never outside an individual's power to change. To me, if you feel something is the right thing to do, there's only one option: you commit to doing it. I was sixty-one years old in 1995, but ever since grade school when I'd taken to hauling my wiry mutt Toffee up into a shaky tree house to help me eat my PB&J sandwiches, I'd always wanted to train a dog to do something special. Thus, I was drawn to SAR. There are many types of canine SAR—cadaver search, water search, avalanche search, wilderness search—and each requires unique training. Disaster search is where the dog searches for live victims trapped in a structure collapse or crashed vehicle or landslide or any other event that might shield victims from the eyes of rescuers. Most important in my mind, in disaster search, my dog and I could potentially *save* a life—about as special a purpose as I could think of.

I had four boys already in college and was just starting a casual retirement with my husband, John, but it probably surprised no one when I shrugged it off and instead quite literally found a spot on the bus in the company of Federal Emergency Management Agency's (FEMA) Los Angeles Urban Search and Rescue (USAR) Task Force. They needed canine disaster search teams, and I had a well-trained Black Lab. So on the morning of April 21, 1995, while the rest of the shocked world mourned the victims of the Oklahoma City bombing, I gathered up Murphy and boarded the shuttle with the first wave of disaster USAR workers.

It was taking us longer to get off the bus than the drive from our staging area at the Myriad Convention Center, where the FEMA USAR Task Force organized late the previous night. We knew the damage to the Alfred P. Murrah Federal Building was extensive. The perpetrator, Timothy McVeigh, had detonated nearly five thousand pounds of homemade explosives, which lifted nine stories of the federal building into the sky and pancaked them down in a 460-ton avalanche, killing 168 innocent people. But as the bus had rolled by the front of the building this morning, the rubble hadn't looked too bad. This would be my first major deployment with the now two-year-old Murphy, and the glimpse I caught of the site made me feel a little better. The search might even be *easy.*

I was confident in Murphy's abilities. She'd charged through canine SAR certification required for deployment like the black fur-missile she was. I was even a little excited to see my high-octane dog in action—*if I could just get off the bus!*

Step. Stop. Bump.

I inch-wormed to the bus's front and tried to see out. It looked like the firefighters ahead of me were captivated by something as soon as they exited. Finally, the path cleared and I made my way out the door. Step.

Stop.

The front of the federal building had been a deception. The building's rear—where the bomb had detonated—stared back at me. A massive gouge cut through the long side of the rectangular building like a hemorrhaging wound. Wires and cables and pipes spilled out the side of each room on every floor. The offices that once contained fourteen federal agencies were now a honeycomb of dark, dead caves.

I could only stare back with the horrified reverence usually reserved for soldiers on the battlefield—yes, one human *could* really do this to others. I'd seen ghastly deeds on the news before, but by then there'd always been a rebuke—justice or a good deed—to balance out the bad. But here amid the smoky destruction, there was no justice. There was no good. For the first time in my life, I felt only the chilly shadow of evil.

How could any good come from this?

No one offered an answer as our solemn procession shuffled off the bus.

TWO DAYS LATER, I noticed the young man lingering at the edge of the newly erected fence around the federal building's rubble pile but paid him no mind. I had to stay focused. Almost eleven hours of searching unforgiving debris, and the job was getting tough. Sweat and dust coagulated into a kind of pliable cement that covered my body. It made breathing laborious. It made *thinking* laborious. Only three days earlier I'd been on vacation with my husband in Palm Springs, and now I was walking through hell on earth.

Stay positive, I reminded myself. It was a mantra I would repeat throughout the entire search.

Murphy glanced back at me. She could sense the slightest change in my mood. There is debate about the extent of a dog's emotional facilities, but it is commonly agreed that a dog can pick up any negative emotion from the handler and fixate on it. The constant search, which search dogs view as an enjoyable game, would suddenly become undesirable. A chore. The dog will worry about the handler and stop paying attention to her nose. The search will break down.

I tapped my remaining reserves of mental toughness and kept my emotions stable. My dog was counting on me. The families of 168 innocent souls were counting on us.

Still, I was on shaky ground—in every sense of the phrase. I was a civilian volunteer on the biggest rubble pile I'd ever seen. Up until this point, search and rescue with Murphy had been nothing more than a weekend endeavor, a way to occupy my time between horse rides. We were well beyond casual pastime now. That pungent and unmistakable scent filling my nose was death. Real death.

We finished our search and began the somber march off the rubble and down a narrow, fenced passage to the buses. That's when I noticed the man again.

He'd been hovering around the edge of the fence for a while. Perhaps hours. But as the man saw me approaching, he began to deliberately walk my way.

As he neared, the man raised his arm and held something out to me.

Maybe a card, or flowers, I thought. I was wearing my FEMA USAR Task Force uniform and helmet, so people easily mistook me for a firefighter. They'd been bringing gifts for the first responders to the disaster site for days now.

It wasn't flowers.

Shocked, I looked at the man's face and saw something that will be forever engraved in my memory. I don't remember his physical features; they were overshadowed by the complete devastation in the man's eyes.

He was holding a photograph in his outstretched hand. The photo showed a young woman with raven-black hair and a bright smile. In a quavering voice, he asked, "Have you found her yet?" Almost four days after the bombing, the man was still searching for his young wife.

I felt my stomach enter free fall. I didn't have the heart to explain that the overpressure from a bomb blast can literally turn organic tissue to mush. Or that the bomb had lifted and dropped nine stories of metal and concrete on anyone lucky enough to survive the blast. My dog could indicate with her body language where a deceased victim might be, but any chance of visual identification would be impossible.

I knew the man needed closure. Murphy might not be the answer to finding the remains of this man's wife, but she sure as hell was part of the team that would.

I summoned what was left of my courage and adjusted my glasses. I placed a hand on the man's shoulder and looked him directly in the eye. "We won't leave until we do," I said.

As I let Murphy lead me quietly away, I made a decision. Something good *had* to come from this disaster.

AND SOMETHING GOOD did emerge from the shadow of evil, but not until the winter of 1995, long after all the victims had been accounted for. It started with an idea.

Murphy had performed extremely well in her searches at Oklahoma City. I had seen what was possible with search dogs, and it wasn't only searching for remains of the deceased. Dogs were faster than any artificial technology at finding live people buried in rubble. With enough trained dogs in enough places, they had the potential to put human lives back on the board when disaster struck.

But my research indicated there was a severe shortage of search dogs—fifteen at the time, only a tiny fraction of the number I estimated were needed. If another large-scale disaster hit the United States, live victims trapped in rubble could be left behind. How would it be if that man's wife had survived the building collapse only to perish because search teams did not have the assets to find her fast enough? In my mind, that was unacceptable.

It would take a massive effort to overcome the search dog deficit. Canine disaster search training and certification would have to be revolutionized. At the time, the majority of search dog training was volunteer-run. Egos and politics were rampant, and time constraints often slowed the process to years. Five years for a trained dog was not uncommon.

A new, *ahem*, breed of dog handler would also need to be instituted—someone with disaster response instincts beyond what weekend warriors could provide. Someone with the mental fortitude to endure the shock of a major disaster and look a victim's family in the eyes afterward.

Above all, the right dogs would need to be selected. I knew Murphy was special. I would need more like her. Dogs that could focus on a single scent amid the chaos of a disaster site, dogs that had the stamina of a professional athlete, the fearlessness of a soldier, the cunning intellect of an escape artist, and the compassion of a nurse. But top-bred dogs matching these characteristics could cost in the thousands of dollars, and for what I had in mind, they'd have to be free. Or damn close.

On the surface, my plan might've appeared impossible. I heard a number of doubtful assessments. But feasibility and popularity played little part in my decision to proceed. It was, after all, the right thing to do.

Only a few months after our return, I created the

National Disaster Search Dog Foundation (SDF). The nonprofit was based on the notion that I could redefine canine disaster search teams in America. What the outside world did not hear was my unspoken goal: in my lifetime, 168 search dog teams would be trained—one for every victim of the Oklahoma City bombing.

With only my loyal Labrador and a tacit resolve as my guides, I began to lay out the blueprint for finding the dogs that would make history.

Three

FINDING THE TALENTED MISFITS

The rubble of Oklahoma City was still vivid in my mental rearview when I began considering training rescued dogs to be search dogs.

It was early 1996, and I was struggling to get my newly minted National Disaster Search Dog Foundation off the ground. I had two friends volunteering part-time as my staff. The budget for our nonprofit was essentially the money left in my savings account, and the donations from a few friends. The road ahead would be a long one if I planned to train one search dog team for every victim in Oklahoma City. I knew the first step in following my vision would be finding the right dogs. Simple on paper, but infinitely complex in practice.

Murphy would've been a great model if I could pay for professionals to breed and select dogs, but that's thousands of dollars our nonprofit didn't have. My foundation would need every penny for *training* dogs, not purchasing them. Donations to a new nonprofit without a proven track record were unlikely. My only option would be taking dogs that nobody wanted: The rejects of the service world. The homeless strays. The unadoptables.

Rescuing misfit service and shelter dogs would obviously be a benevolent move, but the option was risky at best. If I wanted successful search dogs, I would have to keep my emotions in check and make unbiased assessments to ensure every dog met every standard for selection.

IT TOOK ME almost seven years of hard training to develop what I would call a master's-degree-level of knowledge on canine disaster search. I felt confident when it came to recognizing good search dog candidates. Still, I couldn't say with certainty that rescue dogs would be able to become disaster search dogs. And if they could, would I be able to replicate success 168 times? Most rescue dogs go through so much, physically and psychologically, would they even have enough left to make it through training?

For a search dog, the nose is vital. There's no getting around that fact. But the ability to follow a scent trail is only the beginning. Just because a dog can smell it, doesn't necessarily mean the dog will want to *find* it. To seriously consider rescue dogs as candidates, I would need to screen for the dog's prey drive—their ability and willingness to seek out a target, usually a thrown toy, again and again and again without fail. Completing the game and earning the toy would have to be their Holy Grail. We could then shape that drive into seeking a trapped human.

The other critical ingredient I would have to screen for would be physical ability. One reason my Murphy was such an extraordinary search dog was her physical gifts. She had the agility of a gymnast. She could flow over rubble piles like black water. The hourglass is turned for a victim as soon as the building falls or the car crashes. Speed can mean life. Any rescue dogs I considered would have to match Murphy's agility and stamina on a rubble pile without hesitation, and have the drive to repeat the task multiple times. And these qualities would only get the candidate into the stadium, not out onto the playing field. The final ingredient—the make or break factor—was somewhat less tangible.

I'd learned firsthand that disaster sites were only one level north of hell. You're dealing with Mother Nature's wrath or the equally sinister artificial equivalent. Anything stepping into that world inherits chaos and confusion. There'd be helicopters and airplanes transporting teams or circling the disaster site. Heavy machinery clearing rubble. Power tools and breaching equipment screeching and clawing away at blocked passages. Screams and yells, tears, injured victims, dead bodies.

I remember on my first day searching the Oklahoma City debris field, Murphy and I and our partner team happened into a collapsed room of the building's lower floor. The neutral gray and tan tones characteristic of most federal office paint schemes gave way to vibrant blues and yellows. The debris started to contain shattered plastic of other bright colors. At first I was perplexed. Had we somehow wandered into a neighboring children's toy store? Murphy gave a hesitant alert bark, meaning she'd located human scent, but the victims were deceased. The terrible reality set in. We were in the building's preschool. Nineteen of the bombing's victims had been children.

I don't care how prepared you think you are, something like that will hit you like a hammer. Such experiences weigh heavily on handlers, and in turn, weigh heavily on their search dogs. This was the area I had perhaps the greatest concern for training rescues. There'd be no room for skittish behavior or ebbing will in a search dog; lives depend on her maintaining focus on her target, her prey. Successful search dogs need to maintain that amped-up prey *hyper*drive that never wavers even against the most extreme distractors. Not many dogs are built this way— rescues *or* professionally bred.

My initial tests could weed out rescues that didn't possess basic prey drive and physical ability, but the true measure of the dog probably wouldn't be realized until advanced training, where more of a disaster's chaos could be simulated. In other words, I would have to trust my intuition if candidates passed the basic tests and try to see a level deeper—if the dog had the grit and heart to handle a disaster search. Add all of these requirements together and we're talking about 1 percent of dogs in America.

AS THE WINTER of 1996 thawed to spring, I had yet to find a single candidate. I was running out of time and options. Risky as it might be, if rescue dogs had what I thought was the right stuff for the SDF, I would have to trust my instincts and roll the dice.

If I was wrong, and my foundation's first team of dogs failed in training, my vision would likely die on the vine.

Four

PRINCESS ANA

had little time for further deliberation because I soon received a call from Bonnie Bergin, the executive director of the Assistance Dog Institute, an organization in Rohnert Park, California, that trains canines to assist disabled persons. The director told me about Ana, a one-year-old Golden Retriever who'd been surrendered at least twice and was now terrorizing the wheelchair-using individuals she was supposed to be training to assist.

A picturesque Golden, Ana was the color of butterscotch in the sunshine. She had a narrow face with elegant curves. Her small ears fell evenly and lacked the wonky Dumbo-the-Elephant look of some puppies. Her hair always seemed to lie in an orderly fashion, like she'd just been groomed. Proud in an almost regal way, she gave the impression that she sat where she wanted, not where someone told her to. Painted as a portrait, Ana would have seemed to have it all. In the flesh, she was beyond control.

A product of unregistered breeding, the wily pup had been relegated to her original owner's backyard almost immediately. But high fences were only minor setbacks—Ana could jump them. Flower beds? Ana would turn them inside out. Her destructive habits weren't just total, they were constant. Subsequent owners, who'd been fore-warned and believed they were prepared for the storm, were sent reeling. One owner watched in horror as Ana didn't hesitate to chase a toy ball down a cliff face, and then climb back up again.

In short, Ana's future was dim. Dogs surrendered mul-tiple times often find themselves in kill shelters, where limited space and resources mean a short wait for the eu-thanasia needle. An estimated 3.3 million dogs enter shel-ters every year. Even near the new millennium, many shelters were still putting down around 60 percent of the animals they took in.

Ana caught a break when she came to the attention of the Assistance Dog Institute. They saw potential in the puppy and scooped her up to start their training program to be a disability-assistance dog—a service dog that helps physically disabled owners with everyday tasks. Intelligent, driven dogs are important for helping anyone with disabilities, but they also need a governor. Ana was stuck on full-throttle. It didn't take long for the institute to realize its mistake, but the director didn't want to put Ana back in an unprepared home or shelter. She saw raw talent in the dog as long as the energy was properly channeled. She'd heard of my SDF pilot program and hoped I'd be willing to make the seven-hour drive up to check the pup out.

At first, I hesitated. Golden Retrievers are inherently goofy dogs. Long before I'd even conceived the notion to start my foundation I was told I didn't have enough of a sense of humor for Goldens. But Ana sounded like she had a heart full of bottled lightning. Exactly what I needed. Sense of humor be damned. I told the director I'd be there in the morning.

THE NEXT DAY as I drove, I tried to keep my expectations in check. Ana might have developed bad habits that couldn't be trained out of her. She might've developed mental blocks she wouldn't be able to overcome. I reminded myself that this dog had to be a home run for the sake of the SDF. Nonetheless, I also had two promises to keep.

First, Ana would never need to be rescued again. I couldn't have been more than six years old in 1939, the end of the Great Depression, when ten million Americans were slowly finding work again. Yet I distinctly remember my grandmother collecting spare change in an old soup can in her home's tiny kitchen in Newark, New Jersey. The coins would become a weekly donation to the less fortunate. "There are poorer people than us," she would say with a knowing smile. The lesson stuck with me when I started the SDF. There's always someone less fortunate, animals included. So I made the pledge that once I rescued a dog, it would never see the inside of a shelter again, even if it didn't make the cut to be a search dog. If Ana wasn't up to the task, I'd make sure she found a loving home that could handle her. It might take some time, but that was a promise I could keep.

The second promise was more daunting, but it was the one I made to myself when I'd started the SDF in the first place: I had 168 souls to honor. I was stepping out into an abyss but inexperience would be no excuse. I had to take all comers if I wanted to see my goal through.

As my car sped north, I prayed Ana would somehow understand this promise. I needed her as much as she needed me.

AS I TURNED onto the private drive, I had to stifle a laugh. The trek had taken the majority of the day and the sun was starting its descent in the west, spilling a twilight gold over the green hills and across the valley. Four hundred miles north of my home in Ojai, California, the outskirts of Rohnert Park looked more like fabled pastures for horses than a haven for working dogs. Here, the knobby hills of the Sonoma Coast met the moisture skimming off the Pacific Ocean that contributed to the long stretches of fertile plains and helped spawn the grapes of the world-famous Sonoma County wines. About an hour up the 101 from the cramped cityscape of San Francisco, Rohnert Park had many developments springing up and was beginning to meld with the city of Santa Rosa.

The Assistance Dog Institute had its own facility in the city, but the executive director, Bonnie, had invited me to her small ranch where she kenneled the canine candidates—Ana included—for the institute. The ranch sat a few miles west of any urban development where the emerald hills were testament to the coast's extra moisture, and no doubt kept the horses happy. The air was thick with grass pollen and the smell of manure.

The horses weren't the only ones who were happy. As I slowed, the field on my left, once a horse pasture, now held a different type of herd. Sprawled out across the dirt and crab grass, in every lounge position possible, were about twenty-five Golden Retrievers catching the end-of-day sun. They didn't have a care in the world. They all wore the contentedness of a post-Thanksgiving meal and paid me little mind. None of the pack moved, save a few yawns. Except for one dog.

In the middle of the pasture was a remnant of a large tree. It lacked foliage and the skyward-reaching branches of a live tree, but still sported the thick, snaking limbs of the old oak it once was. On a spanning limb, at least five feet high, a new type of foliage had sprouted. Stretched out on the branch, casual and careless, was a slender puppy. The pup was at ease with her elevation, letting her tail lull off the side of the branch like a lounging jaguar in the jungle. The comical jungle cat stand-in stirred my hopes. That was exactly the type of balance and agility and ease in an unfamiliar environment I needed in a search dog. If that was Ana, her perch told me exactly what I needed to know about the dog's physical prowess. I wouldn't even need to test her agility; only her prey drive would remain a question.

BONNIE LED ME to a long wooden barn adjacent to the converted pasture, asking questions about my foundation. Her questions were polite, but held a suspicious edge. This wasn't a blind donation, but an interview. Bonnie was the real deal when it came to raising and training service dogs. She'd created the Assistance Dog Institute, an organization that would later grow into a full-fledged university granting degrees in Human-Canine Services. She would also lead programs that helped rehabilitate inmates of San Quentin State Prison by training them to work with dogs. She wouldn't let her dogs go to just anyone. Adopting a dog—or any living creature—means you inherit the responsibilities of protecting that living being. Ask any dog owner. The dog becomes your four-legged child. And you don't trust your children to just anyone, even if that child is a handful. Bonnie was just being a good dog mom protecting her young. She was hopeful Ana and I would be a good fit, but she was watching me, making sure Ana was going to get the care she deserved. If our roles had been reversed, I would've done the same. I needed to pass this interview if I wanted Ana to be put in my custody.

"LET'S GET THEM dinner," Bonnie said and threw her weight into the large sliding barn door. The sound woke the herd. In an instant, two scores of Golden Retrievers came stampeding into the barn. Instead of charging us, though, the dogs sprinted to the outer edge of the barn and began circling us in an amber cyclone—a gleeful victory lap before dinner.

"Now," Bonnie said, watching the spectacle with an amused smile. "Which one do you think I have in mind for you?"

Now that was a helluva question to ask! A playful challenge, sure, but I heard the test in her voice. I glanced out into the pasture at my only clue. The oak tree stump was bare. Somewhere out in that swirling chaos was the tree-climber, and somewhere out there was my Ana.

For a moment, I stood flummoxed and speechless. In the back of my mind, the needs of the SDF tapped an impatient foot. We needed 168 dogs and had zero. There were currently no other candidates. Bonnie would be sympathetic—our arrangement would be best for Ana, and she wanted it to work out—but that wouldn't make her any more likely to release the dog to an unqualified individual. I stared out into the Golden Retriever merry-go-round. The dogs blended together, nose to tail in a solid blur.

Then Ana quite literally threw me a bone. One of the circling dogs snatched up a stick from the ground and shook it merrily as she trotted around with it. A few of the others tried to clamp on as well but she shook them off. It was like a giant flare had been shot into the sky. Now there was a high-spirited dog with prey drive. It had to be Ana. I went all in.

"Well," I said, pointing to the stick holder, "that's got to be her."

Bonnie slapped her leg. A gleeful spark appeared in her eyes. I'd just moved up a notch or two in her mind. More important, I'd passed the interview. "That's right!" she said. "And believe it or not, she likes to climb trees!"

IT WAS A triumphant drive home with Ana. I was flying high. The foundation was off and running. I would need two more dogs and then I could begin my pilot program, but—call it faith or just stubborn confidence—I was certain after the first dog the floodgates would open. Ana would stay with Murphy, John, and me at our small house in Ojai, and I would set about seeking out my next candidate.

I pulled Ana out of her crate. She stretched into a few long yoga poses then pranced out like she was a newly crowned princess stepping out of her chariot. I walked her up the driveway and opened the door to her new home. *No more animal shelters, Ana. A stable sanctuary and a regimented training plan await. Welcome to your new h—*

Ana bolted inside.

I knew a great deal about training search dogs, but I still had much to learn about shaping a dog's general behavior. When introducing a dog to a new home, it's best to break each room off, bit by bit in bite-size pieces, slowly acclimating the new dog to the new environment. The idea is to establish a disciplined routine up front and avoid the situation I was about to experience. I'd been so caught up in my rising tide of victory, I didn't realize the wave was about to break. Tsunami Ana had reached full force.

Ana took one look at my tranquil living room and decided it was a playground. She sprinted around tables and chairs, running circles and figure eights, skidding into walls and footrests. Then she went bouncing onto the couch, plowing through pillows like bowling pins. From the couch she leapt to the love seat and went straight up the back of it, tipping the chair over. The circus continued for a good ten minutes. I could do nothing but watch the madness through splayed fingers, horrified.

Murphy seemed just as terrified as I was. From the corner, composed and orderly from years of discipline and training, she looked from me to the Golden rampage and back to me again. If canine physiology allowed, her jaw would've been on the floor. Poor girl. She didn't know I needed two more of these hurricanes.

Five

DUSTY GIRL

The turnout next to Highway 101 outside Salinas, California, was an odd place to meet a dog. As I slowed to a stop at the turnout, dust curled around my station wagon and drifted lazily away across the expansive Salinas River Valley. It was early afternoon, but I almost felt like I was showing up to a midnight rendezvous.

A few weeks had passed since I'd brought Ana home. Word about my pilot program was getting around, and I got a call from a woman at a nearby Golden Retriever rescue. She had another young Golden Retriever who fit the description of a search dog candidate—physically fit and prey-driven—ready to be adopted. Of course I was ready, but when I asked to set up a meeting to see the dog, things got a little strange. The woman was hesitant to set anything up. Finally, she suggested this odd, off-the-beaten-path location to meet.

"Why can't I just see the dog at your shelter?" I asked, confused.

The woman's voice dropped to a conspiratorial hush as she informed me she hadn't reported the dog to her rescue organization yet.

Then I understood. The dynamics of an animal rescue organization can differ from group to group. Some subscribe to different philosophies than others. Animals don't have liaisons or representatives to speak for their species, so it falls on their human caretakers to decide what is best for them—often this is based on emotion rather than logic. In the case of this Golden Retriever rescue organization, they did not want to place any rescues as working dogs.

I'd seen the bias before, but it still surprised me. Yes, true, service dogs have tough jobs. Disaster sites can be dangerous. Any dog we let out onto a debris pile incurs some risk. But the notion that the dogs are seen only as tools, or indentured into some type of forced labor is inaccurate. Unfortunately, in their quest to place dogs in the same category as humans, some well-intentioned groups actually have the opposite effect. Confining a lightning bolt like Ana to a household would be the worst thing for her, even cruel. These dogs *need* the constant challenge of a search or training. There is just no other release valve for their energy. In my twenty years of experience, SDF dogs have never incurred more than minor injuries on a disaster site. We train our dogs thoroughly. We pair the dogs with handlers who love them like their own children and care for them accordingly. It's difficult to convey these sentiments to someone who's unfamiliar with the capabilities of such dogs.

I've dealt with a lot of misguided opinions in my life. One almost steered me away from working with animals altogether. I was the first member of my family to attend college. Originally, I'd wanted to be a vet. But in 1951 when I entered college, I was discouraged by a course catalogue that had no qualms suggesting, because of the physical labor involved, a veterinary career was not suitable for a woman. The small minds who'd compiled this catalogue deemed only two options appropriate: nursing or teaching. Well, I grew up climbing trees and never being picked last in neighborhood ball games, so I felt I got the better deal when, at age seventeen, I joined 124 classmates at Panzer College in East Orange, New Jersey, to pursue a degree in physical education. I never became a vet, but I also never let anyone fully extinguish my love of helping animals—which is why, over forty years later, I picked back up right where I'd left off to start the SDF.

I knew persistence was the key to overcoming bias, or any obstacle for that matter—*Providence moves too.* I was lucky the woman on the phone shared a similar will and knew the SDF was in the dog's best interest. She was going out on a limb for this dog, so a little cloak-and-dagger didn't bother me.

The woman pulled up beside me and opened the crate in the back of her car. Out popped a larger, more muscular version of Ana.

"This is Dusty," she said.

The name did not fit this beautiful, powerful female dog. Her bright auburn coat had a finish of merlot-by-sunset red and elicited more the heroic cowgirl image than a "dusty" hue. Then she did something that worried me. When I approached her with praise, the young pup climbed up my legs and wrapped her front legs around my waist like she was giving me a hug. As cute as this might sound, Dusty's behavior indicated a serious lack of confidence. The embrace was not an *aww-love-you* hug, but a *please-don't-abandon-me-again* clutch. The transformation from the graceful girl I'd seen jump from the car put my heart in a vice. Whatever Dusty had been through, it had shattered her confidence.

The woman knew nothing about Dusty's background, except that she'd been picked up as a stray. No papers, no records. In 2016 alone, an estimated 620,000 dogs entered shelters as strays. A large percentage of strays have no documentation. They can't exactly tell their life stories, so if a dog is picked up without tags or context, things like breed, age, and history will be a mystery. As with children, the early years of a dog's life are crucial. In the first few months—a significant amount of time in puppy years—

dogs develop adaptations to the world around them. They learn who their friends are and how they should behave in certain environments. They learn who, or what, they should fear. Research also shows that dogs raised in positive environments early in life have a much better chance of fully developing their brains. If Dusty had endured a traumatic puppyhood—even just a few weeks' worth—was her mind sound enough to train for disaster search? And if she'd developed some innate fear of something a disaster site could present, would she be able to overcome the condition? There would be no room for anxiety on a rubble pile.

There was no time for anxiety on my part either. For the moment, I could only thank my lucky stars she'd been rescued and focus on the future. I showered Dusty with praise as I quickly ran her through some drive tests. Again, she blossomed into the gallant dog I'd seen earlier. So training might be difficult, but with a positive keel, I was confident Dusty would thrive.

I thanked the woman and saddled the SDF's newest dog into my car and we rode off into the sunset. The SDF had just doubled its ranks.

AT THE TIME, the official SDF kennel was still my house. Dusty would be joining Murphy, Ana, and my husband's (non-search) dog. I managed to avoid the rampage-like introduction Ana had made, but the addition of another strong and strong-willed dog to the pack made for quite a madhouse. It was borderline chaos from sunup long into the night as Ana and Dusty immediately took to competing against each other, running constant races around—and sometimes through—the backyard pool. The air was alive with yips and snorts and barks. It was the beautiful music of my vision becoming reality. I couldn't have been happier. I just needed one more dog.

Six

THE GOOD SOUL

The Ojai Humane Society, my local shelter, answered my prayers with Harley. As a clear demonstration that the universe has a sense of humor, Harley was, of course, another Golden Retriever. Three-of-a-kind breedwise was actually not that surprising. The Golden Retriever breed arose during the nineteenth century in the United Kingdom, where the hunting of waterfowl required a medium-sized dog that was comfortable in water. Because the breed has the natural prey drive and physicality of a hunting dog, as well as intelligence and the ability to adapt well to different environments, Goldens are ideal candidates for search dogs. Their friendly temperament and aesthetic beauty also make them a popular breed among the general public, which, unfortunately, also increases the number of Goldens that are surrendered to shelters or escape and become strays.

Breed was perhaps the only thing Harley would share with his Golden sisters-to-be in terms of temperament. He had incredible prey drive and could really move when he wanted to, but he was more like a steam engine—it took him a while to crank up to full speed. Compared to average dogs, Harley was fast, but when put next to his hyperactive sisters, it sometimes seemed like he needed an accompanying soundtrack of a trombone.

From what we were able to determine, Harley had started as a field trial dog. A field trial is essentially a competition that simulates a bird hunt and requires the tested dog to retrieve a downed "fowl" and return it to the owner. The dogs are then judged on their performance. That may sound simple, but the competition field is almost a half-mile long and involves dense grass, swamp, and water. The dog must be in control at all times and obey commands given by the owner from a distance by hand signals or whistles. Multiple fowls must be retrieved in a given heat in a specific manner. The sport spans the country, and competition for the prestigious national title is fierce. In fact, field trials are viewed as among the most difficult competitions for working dogs. Only the absolute cream of retriever dogs can make it. Harley was not the cream.

He looked more like an alley dog. He was a large male with a coat that didn't quite have the same polyester luster as Ana's, nor the fiery red of Dusty's. His hair stuck up in different directions like he was always doing science experiments with static electricity. The hair around his muzzle faded to white, giving him a look of wisdom and sophistication.

That was also not the case. Harley's thoughts seemed to be much like his movements at times in that they wandered, sometimes slowly. This trait did not bode well when it came to the no-room-for-error standards of competition field trials. Harley was probably admonished for his shortcomings on the field. Not many dogs can learn from constant reprimand, though. The negative feedback only drove a deflating nail into the dog's already fragile confidence. The more frustrated his owner became, the more Harley shrank away. Abuse might have followed. By the time he was surrendered to the shelter, Harley was a shell of his former self.

When I met Harley, it broke my heart to see a dog with such potential so reduced. I have my own opinions about an owner who would bully such a kind being, but none that are suitable for print. But Harley has an engine for a heart. He was absolutely committed when I sent him after toys and gave him praise. When you showed you believed in him, he exuded the dedicated loyalty of a soul willing to do anything for his partner. That's what I loved most about him—he was a good soul. I didn't care about his confidence issues. I knew a gentle hand could guide him back to the great dog he was.

WITH FOUR DOGS—three of whose energy multiplied their presence exponentially—Harley would have to be housed elsewhere. I was recommended another dog trainer who had a kennel. The man was a former police dog trainer and had given me advice on dog selection in the past. Unfortunately, I was taught another hard lesson.

The sentiment that dogs should never have to leave the living room couch, much like what I'd seen from the organization where I'd adopted Dusty, also has a polar opposite. It could be referred to as "old school" training methods, but I think of it more as outdated. It is the idea that dogs are not assets or teammates, but rather equipment that needs to be controlled. If the equipment does not perform how you want it to, you fix it, physically. It is what Jack London called "the law of the club." Unfortunately, in some places, this way of thinking had remained prevalent.

A few days after boarding Harley at the kennel, I arrived early to pick him up for his day of training. The man who was boarding Harley tried to force him into a dog run, but the big guy refused to cooperate. I watched in horror as the man lifted his leg and planted a kick in Harley's rear—the absolute worst thing that could be done to the dog.

I'm not a big woman. I don't like to fight. But as I've mentioned, when it's the right thing to do, I don't stay idle. I don't remember exactly what happened next. I do know that Harley was back in my house that night and would never return to the kennel again.

SO MY HOUSE came to have three prime search dog candidates bouncing off the walls like renegade Ping-Pong balls, but I had my pilot program team. Three rookies, primed and ready. Ana, the youngest and smallest, was perhaps the sharpest. She was my ace. I'd seen nothing that might indicate she'd have trouble with training, but you don't know until you try. Dusty, a bit older and more robust, was literally right on her tail. I couldn't see her having any problems with the physical demands of training, but her confidence issues worried me. Would they come back to haunt her? And then there was Harley, my gentle soul. He could plow through the physical portion of training and ask for seconds most likely. But how would he handle the mental demands of constant commands, environment changes, and other stressors? Did he have hidden mental triggers like Dusty? Had the harsh treatment he'd experienced left insurmountable scars?

I had a rejected guide dog, an abused stray, and a washed-out competition dog. Now I had to turn them into the best disaster search dogs America had ever seen.

Seven

ENTER THE MASTER TRAINER

na, Dusty, and Harley—in terms of their combination of physical ability and prey drive—were in the top percentile of dogs in America. But in a way, finding them was the easy part. Now we had to turn their raw talent and energy into usable search skills. This task would depend on more than just optimistic persistence. There are so many trying aspects of disaster search training, even the most robust candidates can fall short. As training stood in 1996, only about 20 percent of dogs made it to become qualified search dogs. For the SDF pilot program, I didn't have any leeway. I needed all three Goldens to pass. I figured that was the minimum for demonstrating SDF training was foolproof. I also did not have the funds to support a backup plan.

I had another problem. Murphy's success had been the result of learning from years of trial and error, dead ends, and inadequate training. If I wanted to get anywhere close to my goal—and thus anywhere close to closing America's gap of search dogs in my lifetime—competent search dogs would have to be regularly produced in under one year. I thought I knew the woman who could do it.

IN 1988, MY first attempt at training a search dog was with Topa, my lanky German Shepherd. When I started training her, the notion to train a dog to do something special had been my only lodestar. Truth be told, I had no idea what I was doing. As it turned out, I wasn't alone.

Every week, I'd load up Topa in the car and drive to the nearest canine SAR club. There were a few different groups, and I bounced from one to the other, trying to soak up as much knowledge as possible to mold Topa into a competent search dog. What's the best reward? Some said toys, others treats. One group heeled the dog on the right, while the other heeled the dog on the left. When I brought up these discrepancies, they were dismissed. I came to realize there was only one common thread across all of these groups—they hated each other.

Before my time, the canine SAR groups in Southern California had started as one. But dog trainers are often hardnosed, type-A personalities. When they give a command, they're used to being obeyed. You can see how, when introducing something as intangible as how to best train a search dog, friction could easily develop. And develop it did. Like a nation fracturing into civil war, the group split into different factions. When the dust settled, there were seven different canine SAR training groups across California, eventually known as the California SAR Dog Confederation, all convinced their own particular way was the right way to train a search dog. Understandable, I suppose, but while the groups tried to refine their training philosophies, the dogs often didn't train at all. It took me almost two years and multiple groups, but I eventually realized the groups were more of a social outlet—dinners and drinks and, of course, discounting the other groups' training philosophies. Meanwhile, my Topa wasn't any closer to becoming a search dog.

More troubling was the fact that the groups didn't seem to *mind* the stagnation. The dogs were happy enough training once a month, but that is no way to make progress. Search standards were malleable benchmarks the groups arbitrarily created. When the majority of the dogs couldn't meet certain time or detection standards, the group sometimes lowered the standard. The groups seemed oblivious to the fact that we were not doing anyone any favors, especially the search dog community. Incompetent dogs and handlers betray a dog's potential. Many rescuers at the time did not, in fact, trust dogs, or figured there were better, more reliable search tools. I couldn't blame them. I would only want the best if my family were trapped under the rubble, wouldn't you? No way would I invest in an asset that might miss a victim.

To make matters worse, the separate groups were convinced the other groups were doing things wrong, so any suggestion otherwise was considered treasonous. I often worried I was being purposefully held at the same level as others—if my dog was to get too good at searching, it would make the others look bad, of course. I couldn't make sense of such behavior—this wasn't a competition or corporate business. Our only goal should've been to save lives.

There were plenty of dogs that would never make good search dogs, but that didn't make them bad dogs. The same went for handlers and trainers—these weren't bad or unskilled people just because their dogs weren't progressing. But these people had invested so much time and energy and money into their dogs, they could no longer detach their egos and look at the end goal of disaster search. They were missing the forest for the trees. They say great humans are too often admired only in retrospect—who knew that applied to great dogs!

In terms of getting Topa trained, the writing was on the wall. She was getting older and beyond the best time to learn new behaviors. I knew something had to change.

———

IN 1991, I switched groups again. Every month, I made the drive up to Bakersfield, California, to meet with a group known as the California Swiss Search Dog Association. I was relieved to find a more progressive atmosphere, focused on furthering the dogs' abilities. They were a smaller group of motivated people, and they adhered to the Swiss disaster search standards, one of the highest standards at the time. The group actually seemed to move toward achieving them. My relief was short-lived.

It didn't take me too many two-hour drives to understand that at the once-a-month pace we were training, Topa might be a certified search dog by the time she reached her Golden years. I can't say at the time I had an accurate notion of the impact search dogs could have on a disaster—I wouldn't until Oklahoma City—but I wanted a competent search dog before I hit *my* Golden years.

Some of the more serious members of the group felt the same. The group's leader used his connections in Switzerland to organize a contingent of Swiss disaster search dog handlers to come visit for a few days and run us through a boot camp of sorts. The Swiss handlers were more than happy to come help our group out, impart their knowledge, and do some import-tax-free shopping for climbing gear at the California-based Patagonia company. We made great progress, and we repeated the boot camp the following year. By 1992, Topa was retired and I had a very young Murphy by my side. Murphy and I ate up the training. In the few weeks the Swiss trainers were with us, I learned more than I did in my entire career as a handler.

Murphy started gaining momentum. It was a treat to see her in her element, searching faster and faster. I knew she was good. The Swiss trainers confirmed she was good. I didn't want to let my foot off the gas pedal. I decided Murphy needed professional coaching from a trainer who knew dogs inside and out and could leave her ego on the sidelines. The obvious choice was the same woman who'd helped me pick Murphy. She was something of a legend in dog-training circles. Her name was Pluis Davern.

PLUIS (PRONOUNCED "PLOUSE") greets newcomers delicately and politely with a small hint of an accent, a remnant of her Dutch upbringing, youth in New Zealand, and university in Australia before her arrival in New York in 1964. Her cautious smile and testing-the-water small talk first give the impression of shyness. This couldn't be further from the truth.

Pluis started her career in dog training almost as soon as she was born. As a young child in 1945 Holland, as the chaos of World War II subsided, she found a strong German Shepherd as a reliable companion. As early as she can remember, she was fascinated with how dogs learned. So she did some learning of her own. The pages of Konrad Lorenz's *Man Meets Dog* became her bible. Her passion never waned. A casual sit-down discussion recounting a dog's behavior often results in Pluis launching herself out of her chair with animated descriptions. She is quick to comment on how she would be up at 6:00 a.m. and training dogs for free if she could still feed her family.

Her passion translated professionally. In 1967 she started her own training business, which would become Sundowners Kennels, near Santa Cruz, California. She quickly branched into several types of dog training, rooted in her insatiable appetite for knowledge about dogs. I hesitate to call her a dog whisperer as it would almost sell her skills short. She is a dog *communicator*. She has trained show dogs, hunting dogs (referred to as gun dogs), field trial dogs, police dogs, and search dogs of all varieties. She has trained champions and won titles. Early in her career, she put on a full-spectrum gun dog seminar and exposé—one of the first of its kind—so eye-opening for those in the sport it was written up in numerous magazines and even a book. She has been awarded "Trainer of the Year" by *Dogs in Review*, and "Breeder of the Year" by the American Kennel Club. She has judged for both the American Kennel Club and the Westminster Dog Show. She often travels worldwide as a guest judge at field trials and show dog championships. In short, she knew what the hell she was doing.

After so much success in the show and gun dog communities, Pluis decided to try to give something back. So she took her champion obedience and field trial dog and partnered with a local vet to train him as a SAR dog. The shift in focus wasn't difficult as much of field trials and SAR share idiosyncrasies. Pluis herself was a certified search dog handler and had deployed locally in support of small disasters. I couldn't think of a better partner in crime.

THE FIRST TIME I showed up at Pluis's kennel near Santa Cruz she had me run through a few commands with the dog. I finished what I thought was a flawless routine of basic obedience and looked at her for what I expected would be glowing praise.

She gave me an amused smile and with the humor that always sneaks into conversations, said, "Well, your dog's got *you* well trained."

That didn't sound like praise to me. I started to worry. I needed to get my dog up to speed for the certification test.

"Go away," Pluis said with a smile. "I'll work with the dog for a month. Then we'll see."

So I did. When I came back, it was like I had a different dog. Pluis had turned on a light for me. I began to understand what she meant by the dog training me. In an effort to get the dog to succeed, a handler will subconsciously compensate for the dog in certain behaviors. For example, if I gave Murphy a sit command, maybe she would start to sit, yet her haunches not actually touch the ground, but since she got the main idea of the command

I would still reward her. And while cutting corners might slide by in obedience training, on a real search it could amount to missed victims. It was a lesson I would apply to Murphy to turn my spunky Black Lab into a searching machine.

By 1993, thanks to Pluis's guidance and training, Murphy was excelling on the rubble pile. I could tell what an incredible asset Pluis would be to a search organization. She became my first stop for everything. I would drive the five hours up to Sundowners Kennels, feeling like I'd uncovered buried treasure.

I figured everyone from the search groups would be thrilled to soak in her wisdom. I brought my new skills and my dog's ever-growing success back to the search group. I expected a warm reception. What I got surprised me, to say the least. My suggestions for bringing in Pluis to train the group full-time were ignored. Training ideas I knew worked for my dog were dismissed, especially by the upper ranks of our organization, as if they did not want to cede any power in any form to another training ideology. I was flabbergasted. Why, I thought, if it is for the greater good, would anyone even think of standing in the way?

When I brought the situation up to Pluis, she nodded as if she knew the scenario all too well. "You know," she said with a sad smile, "in the show ring, I had a lot of friends until I started winning." The numbers didn't lie. Under the California SAR Dog Confederation, the seven subgroups had produced only one dog at an advanced level in 1994, and subsequent years hadn't seen much better results.

In my opinion, the people were failing, not the dogs. I was not willing to accept that. So I did what I had to do and started my own group. It was the precursor to the Search Dog Foundation, but it held the same general principles I would later adopt for the foundation. The few individuals from other groups who wanted to share in my new knowledge followed me. Pluis became our sage adviser and go-to trainer. She affectionately called me "the little bulldozer" because all I did was push forward. What neither of us could see was how intertwined we were to become over the next two decades and what we would accomplish together.

Eight

TRAINING BEGINS

Pluis did not need much convincing to get on board with training shelter dogs to be search dogs. The obsessive prey drive that made the dogs unmanageable in an average family's living room was exactly what she wanted in a potential search dog. So in early 1996, I delivered Ana, Dusty, and Harley—my brilliant misfits—to Pluis, hoping for the same transformation she'd engineered with Murphy.

Unlike me, who didn't exactly share their sense of humor, Pluis loved Goldens. Pluis had adopted one with an impressive lineage as the family dog when they moved to California. Pluis knew how to handle the energy and trained her Golden into a champion obedience dog.

Pluis learned how deeply hunting was embedded in retriever genetics, so she learned how to do it herself. For Christmas, her husband bought her a Beretta 12-gauge shotgun. Pluis was ecstatic, but her family in Holland didn't share her enthusiasm. *You got an instrument of death at Christmastime?* was her mother's horrified response. Undeterred, Pluis bred the dog and trained one of her puppies into a champion gun dog and field trial dog.

When Pluis found out my pilot program dogs were all Goldens, she was overjoyed. She sees them as thinking dogs, but in their own unique way. Where Labradors and Border Collies usually stay well within the rules and follow a specific pattern of behavior, Goldens will adjust their behavior depending how they feel in the moment. She admiringly refers to them as the "anarchists of the dog world." If anyone knew how to channel the special "anarchy" of a Golden into something special in itself, it was her.

Pluis structured her search dog training in a manner similar to that for a field trial dog. After all, they're both hunting and retrieving in a sense, and both types of dogs have to be strictly controlled.

The first phase of training was a calming stage consisting of basic obedience training—simple commands and tasks to establish a structured routine for the dogs. For these intelligent dogs, basic obedience was something they could accomplish easily and establish a base to build on. For Dusty and Harley, this was also a great opportunity to beef up their confidence. Like a pro basketball player working on dribbling, they could develop confidence in fundamentals that would translate into confidence in the advanced stages.

Basic obedience also was an outlet for the dogs' endless energy. Ana was the key benefactor here—every morning a small nuclear reactor spun to life in her chest. If she wasn't allowed to defuse, you'd have a small nuclear meltdown on your hands. Pluis had the leash bruises to prove it.

The other element of the first training phase was to get the dogs familiar with the unstable and unpredictable environment of a disaster site. This meant exposing the dogs to different surfaces and obstacles. As Pluis puts it, "They need to be relaxed enough to stand on their pads, not their claws, and shift weight on rubble if it moves. This is the best way to prevent injuries. Properly trained dogs can walk on nails and broken glass and stay safe even without booties."

We didn't have rubble piles to work with, but we did have a multitude of surfaces and obstacles. Pluis's training area was something of a doggy circus ring. There were simple obstacles—wide tunnels with open ends, and horizontal ladders with round rungs that lay on the ground. There were advanced obstacles—curving tunnels with no clear opening or exit, A-frame ramps, teeter-totters, elevated ladders, and balance beams. Then there were the hero-level obstacles. First was a steep ladder with narrow rungs, approaching a seventy-five-degree incline. These ladders would lead to a balance beam that would make a seasoned gymnast cringe—less than four inches wide with a six-foot drop on either side. Next was a sway bridge consisting of a two-by-four suspended by chains a few feet high; the bridge would rock back and forth once a dog mounted it. This obstacle was more of a psychological challenge for a dog used to being on solid ground.

But the final obstacle was what really separated the dogs from the puppies. Known as "the wobbly monster," it was an elevated bridge-like contraption, but instead of a walkway, it had separate boards as footholds, no wider than a quarter. The footholds stuck up like uneven piano keys, and each would teeter back and forth depending on how pressure was applied. The obstacle required mastery of the instability of the suspended bridge, the fine accuracy of the fire ladder, and the awkwardness of a balance beam all at the same time, while adding in an element of timing. A dog not only had to move correctly, but also had to move at the right time.

Each of these obstacles matched an element a search dog would see on a rubble pile. A handler often sends out a search dog on its own—dogs are much faster without a clumsy human hanging onto the leash, and need to have the skills and confidence to move with ease independently. The ladders in the obstacle course corresponded to fire ladders used in rescues to ascend to multistory buildings. The dogs would need to climb them. Tunnels matched the natural tunnels often formed by voids in rubble. A human couldn't fit in these tight quarters, so it was up to the dog. The balance beams and the sway bridge corresponded to I beams or narrow pathways spanning gaps in a rubble pile. Balance on these obstacles would allow swift passage over rubble of varying heights and prevent dangerous falls.

Even the teeter-totters and the wobbly monster serve a pragmatic purpose. Very rarely are all pieces of debris on a rubble pile stable. They buck, break, or shift under varying loads, and on earthquake sites, rescuers often face aftershocks that cause the same effect. If a dog leaps onto an unsecured slab of concrete, maybe with another piece of debris acting as a fulcrum, that slab will start to tip like a teeter-totter. If the dog panics and tries to bail out, she could land in an injury-causing position or a more dangerous place. If the dog fails to exercise patience and tries to charge forward, she could face a long drop on the other end. However, if the dog recognizes the shift, remains calm, and uses measured timing to guide her steps forward, she can simply ride the teeter-totter down to a smooth landing. That is the bottom line of all these obstacles: teaching the dogs to use their innate abilities to keep themselves safe. If we didn't address it thoroughly in training under controlled conditions, the results in the aftermath of a real disaster could be, well, disastrous.

———

PLUIS STARTED OBEDIENCE training with the pilot program dogs immediately, which was when she hit her first problem: Ana had a bit of an attitude.

For Ana, obedience training was old news from her days as an assistance dog, and she didn't mind letting people know that the commands were not at the top of her to-do list. When Pluis gave a heel command, Dusty and Harley complied without much fuss. Ana, on the other hand, would give Pluis a stare like *I have to do that?*

Pluis would stand firm. "Ana, heel."

A disgusted look from Ana. *Really?*

"Ana, I want you to *heel.*"

Aw, couldn't we just go out there and play?

And so the drama would play out. (Despite the theatrics, Ana actually would not take the cake as prima donna. That title would later fall to an intelligent Border Collie with black tents for ears named Gypsy. When Gypsy was first introduced to the basic obedience commands, the black-and-white pup would actually turn her back to Pluis and face the other direction.)

But Ana could not be doing her own thing on a rubble pile, so Pluis had to keep her grounded. She arranged Ana's training like a mother corralling a rowdy child—Ana would get to go out and play, just as soon as she did her chores. And, with the dog equivalent of I'll-do-it-but-I'm-not-going-to-like-it, Ana complied and improved. Eventually, all three dogs learned to love the program's structure and the opportunity to get some of their angst out every day. As long as each dog's foibles were properly addressed—the gas pedal for Dusty and Harley, the brake for Ana—Pluis saw she wouldn't have any problem obedience-wise with the dogs.

Exposing them to different surfaces, obstacles, and environments was a bit more difficult. Most dogs lack proprioception, meaning they are not spatially aware of where their own limbs are in relation to the surface they are on. To traverse unnatural obstacles like ladders and teeter-totters, the dog must be taught to actually recognize, yes, that's my rear right paw and it needs to go here, and so forth. We already knew all three dogs were incredible physical specimens with off-the-chart agility, so it just would be a matter of coaching their minds to accept the new material.

I do need to clarify. When I say most dogs lack proprioception, I mean most dogs except for Ana, the Tarzan of the canine world. She blew through the beginner obstacles without breaking a sweat, probably because they were nothing compared to the trees she'd scaled in her youth. She would literally prance across the horizontal ladders without any type of instruction, as if she was doing it for fun. Her boastful attitude might've annoyed her kennelmates, but Pluis was at least glad to move past the too-cool-for-school attitude Ana had begun training with. Pluis again focused more on slowing Ana down a bit—ensuring each movement was measured and repeatable—more than actually coaching her in new movements.

Dusty wasn't too far behind. She had wild energy, but needed a little more coaching from Pluis and an under-hand delivery of any corrections. If you raised your voice at all, even if it wasn't directed at Dusty, she would cringe away, worried that somehow she'd done something wrong. Still, one of the godly traits of dogs is their ability to believe in the best of their handler's intentions. With Pluis's gentle guidance and every successful task, Dusty's confidence grew. Soon she matched Ana on skill across the beginner obstacles. She was going to be a force to be reckoned with on the advanced obstacles. Pluis had no real concerns for either dog when the time came to graduate to the wobbly monster.

Having started about a month behind, Harley was not as warp-speed as his sisters, but was still physically gifted. He would glide over the small rock fields and other terrain on Pluis's land without a second thought. But as with a major league ball player who spends too long on deck before batting, when it came to the obstacles, Harley would start thinking too much and psyche himself out. The extra attention and specific commands would stir memories of abuse. The yellow dog with the Golden soul—he knew he could, he just wasn't sure if he *should*.

Pluis knew exactly how to handle such a case. When it came time for Harley to cross the horizontal ladder, footing was not an issue; Pluis would build him up the whole way.

One step.

"Good boy, Harley! Gooooood boy!"

Two steps.

"Great, Harley! Such a goooood boy!"

Three steps. A little faster.

With copious amounts of tender praise, Harley made it across the ladder and through all the other beginner obstacles. He became faster, eventually keeping up with his sisters. And when Harley got something, he really got it. His confidence became less fragile. Pluis was certain she could use the same method to get him over any obstacle. In the corner of the agility course, the wobbly monster loomed.

THE BASIC OBEDIENCE and obstacles phase continued for a few weeks. There wasn't—and really couldn't be—a set time line. The dogs would only move on to the next phase of training when they were ready. But they were getting close.

Pluis kept a training journal for each dog and would rate him or her on specific tasks day by day using a simple system of stars. One star meant the dog needed work. Four stars meant the dog had the task mastered brilliantly. A scrawled ARRHHHHHH was, well, self-explanatory (recently, she has considered moving to emojis). Pluis delighted in giving four stars—it meant her training was working and the dogs were progressing. Ana and Dusty, straight-A students from the onset, were hitting four stars immediately. After overcoming some initial hesitation, Harley was acing the basics as well and even giving his sisters a run for their money on some of the obstacles. Pluis began seeing four-stars across the board and knew it was time for the next phase.

THE NEXT BLOCK of the curriculum involved a forced fetch, or what is sometimes known as the induced retrieve. Pluis would now harness the dogs' excessive prey drive, the obsession over the toy, and shape it into a usable tool on a disaster site. She would teach them that to find one victim is good, but finding two is even better. Such a conditioned response had to be second nature before a dog got out on a rubble pile without a "bribe" of food treats— you couldn't have dogs deciding they don't feel like searching because you forgot your hindquarter of lamb. This phase would also build on the fundamentals, adding more obedience and advanced obstacles.

The casual observer might think that once dogs have mastered a basic obedience skill in their kennel they can perform the task anywhere. After all, human children who learn to eat at the table in the house have no issue eating in a restaurant. This type of transference does not apply to dogs. Dogs cannot extrapolate an experience from one environment into another without training. If you teach a puppy to sit in your house, he'll eventually learn it on command. But take that same puppy out on a walk and try the same command. The first few times the pup will likely have no idea what you want him to do. The dog must be trained on the same task in multiple environments. Although my dogs were sharp, they still had to build up that body of knowledge, so Pluis took them through the same obedience in different situations at different times.

The continual obedience training and exposure to the obstacle course was making a huge impact. All three dogs smashed this phase to pieces; four stars across the board. All three dogs were confident in their abilities. Most important, the dogs loved what they were doing. Counterintuitive as it may seem to humans, disaster search is a simple game for the dog—find person, get toy. Nobody wants to play a boring game, dogs especially. Dogs don't understand the concept of working for a period of time and then relaxing on the weekends. As Pluis put it, "The dog is not thinking, 'I'm going to rescue humanity,' he's thinking, 'Someone out there has a toy!'" We couldn't convince the dog to work hard for weeks on end because at the end of it all he'd get two-weeks' paid vacation in Cabo. Dogs live only in the moment. It's probably something we humans can learn a thing or two from. But in terms of search training, the pace of the instruction had to be doled out in such a way that the dogs were constantly entertained and engaged.

Pluis instituted a proven-yet-not-widely-employed method for enhancing the dogs' comprehension and attention. Many are probably familiar with the concept of latent learning in humans—the idea that it takes time for new teachings to sink in. It's where the expression *let me sleep on it* comes from. Latent learning also applies to dogs. Pluis would take Dusty and teach her a new skill. Once Dusty mastered the command, Pluis would put her in a crate or kennel—somewhere with no stimulus—and let the lesson sink in before pulling her out again. This technique is often overlooked because, at first, it takes much longer to see results. But we were training dog Olympians, not weekend warriors.

Pluis's time investment in the dogs paid off. The previous phase was ground school, now it was time for the dogs to start flying. And fly they did. As more time passed, the dogs' learning expanded exponentially.

Soon Pluis knew the dogs were ready to proceed to the final stage. The dogs were screaming along at this point, on pace to finish in about seven months. This time line was unheard of. If the dogs had been training in karate, they would've entered as white belts, and now, a few months later, be prepping to test for their black belt. We weren't letting the momentum carry us away, but up to this point, Pluis had yet to see any signs of slowing in the dogs. Her only real learning point was that she'd set her initial expectations of the dogs too low. So she borrowed some of my inner bulldozer and pushed forward.

THE FINAL PHASE brought everything together. The dogs would combine all their obedience, agility, and search skills and apply them to the most challenging terrain and obstacles the kennel could offer. The dogs would have to perform these tasks based on signals beyond verbal commands—blows from a whistle or hand signals—given from a handler some distance away (the handler points left, the dogs go left, and so forth). Finally, once a buried victim had been located, the dogs would be required to perform a bark alert—a sustained bark—until the handler reached the location, and not begin searching again until instructed to do so.

To pass the final phase of training, the dogs would have to negotiate all the advanced obstacles. The dogs had been exposed to obstacles of increasing difficulty, but this phase had one key difference—the obstacle had to be performed under complete control, meaning the dog had to mount and dismount safely and on command, stop at any time during the run, and even turn around and go in reverse on certain obstacles. If Ana, Dusty, and Harley could complete these tasks consistently, Pluis would "graduate" them and we'd pair them with their future handlers. We were setting a record training pace for 1996, but this phase was where everything had to come together.

Over the next few months, Pluis began adding more of the final elements into the training. She put the dogs up on a platform at a distance and ran them through the hand signal commands. The dogs picked it up right away. Bark alert after finding a "buried" victim? Ana, Dusty, and Harley had no problems. In fact, they weren't having any difficulties. They were getting faster, more precise. The advanced obstacles were tiny pebbles under their paws. In terms of agility, Pluis had never seen anything like Ana, and Dusty and Harley weren't far behind. Composed and under control, Dusty was climbing up and down ladders. Harley was strutting across the sway bridge, forward, backward, it did not matter, his head held high with confidence. They were banging on the graduation door. There wasn't much more Pluis could throw at them except the wobbly monster.

Nine

THE WOBBLY MONSTER COMETH

By this point, all three dogs had been exposed to the monster. They'd negotiated it to some degree and weren't going in cold. But now they needed poise, control, and complete mastery to convince Pluis they could handle any obstacle on a disaster site.

Dusty climbed the ramp up to the wobbly monster and picked her way across with careful steps. The individual blades rocked back and forth, but Dusty continued, timing each step so the teetering foothold came to rest before moving her next foot, never stretching beyond her balance point. With a steady rhythm, one paw in front of the other, she negotiated the unsteady steps and dismounted, cool as the backside of the pillow. Four stars.

Harley climbed the monster with determination, the shifting steps made his larger frame constantly adjust to avoid losing balance. His big paws curled around the tiny steps like they were going to swallow them up. Too much pressure in a direction too quickly, and the dog would be thrown off balance. Harley did not spook. He advanced across the swaying blades and into a controlled dismount— and an extra helping of praise from Pluis. Four stars.

Ana almost didn't get a second thought from Pluis. The concern wasn't if she could tackle the wobbly monster— she practically warmed up with the obstacle during free play—but if she could do it under control. Pluis didn't want the spry Golden doing flips off it or walking across in a doggy handstand, even if she probably could. Safety, not show, was the point.

Ana started out perfect, smooth and fast, her intensity obvious but securely bridled. She was about halfway across the shifting blades of the monster when she stopped. An onlooker would've almost had enough time for concern— the poor girl froze! Then she tossed Pluis a look like, *Well, how do you like it so far?* She wasn't freezing, she was a gymnast in the midst of a gold medal routine giving a wink to the judges. Then she did something Pluis had never seen in all her years of training dogs. Ana pivoted on the tiny blades of the monster and turned around. She pranced back to the beginning of the obstacle, pivoted once more and completed the entire obstacle again, the apotheosis of composure. Pluis was all but delighted to give her star pupil four stars.

What delighted her more was that these dogs were ready to be paired with their human handlers. Pluis had taken three rescues, written off by the rest of the service dog world, and trained them to be handler-ready in less than eight months—faster than anything seen before. There was still more training to do, but it was clear that any weakness in my pilot program wouldn't come from the dogs. We now needed human handlers that could match the dogs' competence.

Ten

TRIAL BY FIRE

The concussion of boots echoing down the passageway roused me from sleep as the USS *Constellation* aircraft carrier steamed east across the Pacific Ocean in May of 1995.

Oklahoma City was a few weeks old, but in the carrier's tiny sleeping quarters the ghosts of the tragedy still lingered. I still saw the face of the young man whose wife was gone forever; felt the brittle plastic of the crushed children's toys from the day care center; heard the consuming silence as the dead were carried off the rubble pile. The memories flitted in and out of my subconscious, muting my normal happiness.

My eldest son was a navy pilot on the carrier, and as

they finished their cruise, the navy had invited families aboard for the short steam from Hawaii back to California. I wanted to be there on the ship enjoying myself—experiencing what I *should* be feeling—but I just couldn't seem to stay in the present. I kept stumbling on my frustration. Based on my research since Oklahoma City, I knew our country was ill prepared when it came to disaster response and the poor state of readiness baffled me. Beneath it all was a simmering anger searching for an outlet.

And here came the boots thudding closer. I knew what was coming but found myself tensing and recoiling. *thudThudTHUD!*

The curtain around my bed was ripped open by a portly noncommissioned officer. She gave me a this-will-only-hurt-a-bit smile and barked, "Time to get up!"

She'd gone through the same routine yesterday. We'd been on the family cruise for a few days. It was a just-for-fun event, but they still wanted to give us the full huzzah experience of the navy. We had a schedule to keep. I knew this. But for a reason I couldn't quite pin down, her commands were needles under my nails.

My hand shot out and grabbed the curtain from the nonplussed NCO. "I'll get up when I'm ready!" I snapped, and ripped the curtain shut.

IN RETROSPECT, IT'S a funny story. But it brings to light the taxing impact of working in any type of emergency response service. The dogs aren't the only ones who need strong minds in USAR. I didn't realize it, but I'd been experiencing mild post-traumatic stress from my time in Oklahoma City. And in those days, civilians just went home and cried into their pillows. I hadn't been prepared for the horrible things I saw, and I never wanted to see them again. The experience underscored how much death is involved in a disaster. The general public might think search-and-rescue teams run around rubble digging people out a dozen at a time. In reality, the chances of finding someone buried alive are probably a million to one. (If a live victim is found, the actual "digging"—dangerous and excruciating work—is done by a rescue squad that specializes in extraction.) I've known people in USAR who have gone decades without extracting a single live victim. This hard truth was a major factor I had to consider in building the SDF. I couldn't train bulletproof dogs only to have psychologically unprepared handlers who would fall to pieces after every deployment.

Later in 1995, my husband (who, by the way, had slept soundly on our cruise, sharing an officer's quarters with my son up the hall), provided a solution. He'd been in agreement with the grand experiment of the SDF, but he was dead set on one point: the handlers would have to be a blank slate; no dog experience, period. Experience is great, but it's also a double-edged sword. If I wanted the SDF dogs to be the universal standard for success—now and well into the future—there could be no bad habits already set in the handlers.

Most of all, the SDF-trained handlers needed to be professionals. Someone better prepared than the avid hobbyist and weekend warrior, someone better prepared than I myself had been. John insisted on firefighters. His argument had merit. I thought back to the first days of my Oklahoma City bombing deployment, when the Los Angeles County Task Force first met the other first responders at the disaster site. We had four civilian dog handlers and two firefighters on the task force. Our firefighters bonded almost immediately with the other first responders—from what I've seen, wearing the firefighter badge is a bond that transcends just about any social boundary; they know the other has been through the same trials and faced the same adversity. Dogs and civilians were a different story. The firefighters were skeptical of us, and I couldn't blame them. Put yourself in their boots: wade through the dust and wear the sweat of eighteen hours digging through destruction beside your brothers and sisters, and now here comes this retired teacher with gray hair and a dog you've never seen work. Who knew what dues I'd paid, what training I'd completed? Would you trust me as the best tool to find the buried victims of the city you have the responsibility to protect? Of course not. Thankfully, the stigma didn't last—it didn't take many eighteen-hour shifts for the OKC firefighters to accept us as viable members of the team. Still, I learned my lesson. The work wore you down. Murphy had done her job. I, on the other hand, barely made it through, supplementing my dinner every night with ibuprofen. It really needed to be a thirty-year-old firefighter at the end of Murphy's leash.

The more I considered John's idea, the more I liked it. If the conditions on a site are especially challenging— sweltering heat, sharp debris, innumerable distractions— the dogs would need frequent breaks. The rescue operation couldn't stop with the dogs, though; there's always something to be done. As civilians, we were able to help with menial tasks, but largely, when our dogs were down, so were we. Firefighters are trained in emergency medicine, special tools, and other aspects of disaster response invaluable to the effort. So when a handler's dog needed a break, they could go back to assisting another squad, treating wounded bystanders, or any number of the tasks that fall on the shoulders of normal firefighters.

When they weren't deployed, firefighters could continue training regularly. In many ways, dogs are like humans. They like to take the easiest route. If they're not constantly held to high standards, they'll find shortcuts. A handler needs to be up training every day, sharpening the blade. Constant training would make the search teams great and *keep* them that way. A firefighter would be able to fit such a training plan into his or her demanding schedule.

And then there were the psychological reasons. A firefighter probably wouldn't have needed to vent her anger like I'd done on that unsuspecting NCO on the aircraft carrier. Firefighters deal with the aftermath of daily tragedies—the mangled bodies of car crashes, the charred property after fires—all the time. This is not to say it is any easier for them, but they're much better prepared than civilians. Firefighters have a well-oiled support system that allows them to address what they've seen. They can vent their anger or sadness or frustration to professional counselors or comrades and work through it in a positive manner instead of lashing out, like I had done on the cruise. I started searching for dedicated firefighters to be the handlers for SDF pilot program dogs.

AS ANA, DUSTY, and Harley were making their way across the obstacles at Sundowners Kennels, I was negotiating an obstacle course of my own, trying to gain favor with the California Office of Emergency Services (OES) to give me firefighters for my SDF pilot program. It was here I met Mike Antonucci, a man who'd prove to be instrumental in building the foundation.

At the time, Mike was the deputy chief of USAR in California. A career firefighter, Mike had qualified as an EMT while he was still in high school. He'd seen every angle of the firefighter and paramedic role over his forty-plus years of service. He'd also been at the aftermath of the Oklahoma City bombing. He knew how valuable dogs could be to the rescue effort.

The drastic shortage of search dogs had become a hot-button issue for the California OES. Mike's new assignment was to produce the ninety-six dogs the state of

California deemed necessary for emergency readiness. He had been tasked with making the California SAR Dog Confederation groups in the state work better together, once and for all.

Mike was no-nonsense. He was used to the discipline of fire departments, and all the infighting in the civilian canine training groups made his blood boil. He immediately started making changes. The groups lashed out at him just as they had at me. They went to his boss and claimed Mike was "ruining" the canine programs. In reality, Mike was just solidifying standards to better achieve the required FEMA canine SAR certifications.

I was facing a lot of resistance as well. When I'd floated my idea of using firefighters as handlers at a California SAR Dog Confederation meeting, the minutes reflected many "questions raised about whether the SDF would conflict with fundraising efforts of the Confederation" and "using firefighters would usurp the role of the Confederation."

Mike stepping in was a breath of fresh air. I knew he would be open to any improvement, but also that I'd better have my ducks in a row. So I did what anybody does when you need a meeting with one of the highest-ranking OES officials in the state—I kidnapped him.

I SAW MIKE at a FEMA canine certification test we were both observing, and during our lunch break I asked him to come talk about my new idea. "Bring your lunch and we can talk privately in my car," I told him. He agreed, thinking we'd just have a quick chat. As soon as he got in the car, I hit the gas and sped off.

"What are you doing?" Mike asked indignantly, taken off guard at being kidnapped by an old lady.

"Just be quiet and eat your lunch," I told him as I parked. Then I pulled out my laptop and gave him a full presentation on my vision for the SDF. I let him know the dogs wouldn't cost the fire departments a dime. As I finished my pitch, Mike seemed to snap to attention, his eyes alight.

"Wilma," he said with a surprising intensity. "If you want my help, this cannot fail. If the pilot program fails from the get-go, we won't be able to recover. So *I* will choose the first three firefighters."

His response was so abrupt, I was momentarily speechless. *I* was the one thrown off her game. I didn't want the state government getting tangled up in my foundation. Bureaucracy equals a quagmire. I needed lean and mean.

Before I could protest, he continued, "And you need to let me choose those firefighters because it will add credibility to your cause."

Credibility? I hadn't really thought about that. But I would need credibility if I wanted firefighters to buy into a civilian program.

"And, not only that," Mike concluded, "I'll choose departments that are committed one hundred percent and will do what they say."

Departments don't do what they say? That was a new

concept for me. I wouldn't want to be on the receiving end of a department that might change its mind halfway down the road. Dealing with civilian search dog groups had been enough of a hassle. My shock thawed into appreciation.

"Ok, Mike," I said, finding my words again. "I figure out the curriculum, and you choose the firefighters."

I released my hostage and we parted ways, each imbued with an ember of renewed purpose now burning in our brains. He hadn't seen the last of me but at least deserved a reprieve.

THE CALL CAME a few months later, just as I was wrapping up work at my desk in my small home office for the evening. Pluis was progressing well with the dogs. They would soon transition to the final stage and start taking on those advanced obstacles. I knew we were approaching about a month out before we would want to pair the handlers with the dogs. I'd assembled the skeleton of a training curriculum for the handlers and it was enormous. Three weeks straight of classroom work and hands-on exercises with Murphy, then right into ten days with the dogs at Pluis's kennel. I didn't know if the dogs could work for thirty days straight. Hell, I had doubts if *I* could work for thirty days straight.

When I picked up Mike's call, I expected we were about to inherit three Ventura County firefighters, hit the ground running, and never look back.

Mike greeted me with the same enthusiasm as when I'd pitched my idea to him, then continued to read me the names of three firefighters from Sacramento.

What?

"Sacramento?" I gaped. "Mike, I've never even been there. I'm going to have to pull out my map just to be sure where it is."

"Trust me, Wilma," Mike said as casually as if he'd chosen my neighbors as the firefighters, "that's where they are. Those three departments I can count on. And those three guys, I can *really* count on."

He gave me the firefighters' information and hung up. I sat at my desk, dumbfounded. Minutes ticked by as my stunned mind whirled away, uselessly stuck in neutral. Never in a million years would I have believed Mike would pick firefighters outside of Ventura County. It made no sense! We weren't talking about the two-hour drive to Bakersfield here. Sacramento was a good six hours away. I couldn't commute. And I had no budget for a hotel. I would literally have to put everything else in my life on pause, uproot my home, and move there for the training period.

Slowly, my resolve rebuilt my confidence. I'd wanted the best, hadn't I? I'd never mandated the best had to come from somewhere within commuting distance of my home. Mike had held up his end of the bargain. He was taking a big professional risk supporting me. Now it was my turn. If I had to move, so be it. Problem, meet your solution.

I called the firefighters individually and delivered my marching orders. We'd need a rubble pile for search training, an obstacle course for the dogs to train their agility, a central (dog-friendly) meeting place. I gave them a reading list to start building their knowledge. I also made it clear I wouldn't be staying in a motel, so one of them needed to clear off a couch or a spare bedroom—without any navy-type alarm clocks. True to their reputations, the firefighters called back a few days later confirming they'd completed all the tasks. They were ready to go.

THERE WAS ONE order of business I had to tackle before leaving for Sacramento, and it wasn't going to be fun. My splinter group of civilian canine handlers, the ones who'd followed Murphy and me to Pluis, knew I wanted to use firefighters as handlers, but still wanted to be the ones with the new search dogs from the pilot program. They'd been working hard and they wanted the reward. I needed to break the news to them. It wouldn't be easy. I felt for them—I really did. They were doing everything right. They would make good handlers eventually, just not in the SDF pilot program. I had to replicate training beyond the handful of people in my group to meet the needs of our nation.

How I wished otherwise. It was the right thing to do, but the right thing is seldom the easy thing. The handlers-in-training would no doubt be upset. Still, I thought they'd understand the sacrifice. They'd see I wasn't coming to this decision lightly or without reason. So I gathered them up and explained the situation, expecting them to accept the facts like reasonable adults.

They mutinied.

They yelled and screamed and cursed me. I told them I understood their anger, but the decision was made. They packed up and stomped out. I watched them go with a heavy heart. Another bridge burned. At this point, I think the SDF had more enemies than allies. The angry mob again stormed Mike Antonucci's boss, advocating that what I was trying to do was impossible and my program would produce substandard dogs. I could only grit my teeth, believe in my cause, and hope the future would bring the building of new bridges.

A FEW MONTHS later, I packed up Murphy, kissed John, and hit the road, leaving the churlish jibes of my critics behind. Their doubts were grounded in reality. I was radically challenging all pillars of disaster search training. I would be using volatile, renegade dogs, drastically shortened training times, and inexperienced handlers. My doubts could only be conquered by actions. It was time to attempt the final hurdle of the pilot program.

Eleven

THE POOP BAG DECREE

n January of 1997, Murphy and I took over a spare bedroom from Rick Lee, a firefighter from Sacramento, and his wife, Luann. Rick was a guided missile when it came to his job; he would lock on target and not stray an inch. He wore his hair cropped close and his mustache edged sharp. Any task he took on deserved his full effort and had to be done correctly, step-by-step down a mental checklist to make sure all was in order. The only cracks in his armor were gloves—while concentrating on everything else, he often misplaced his gloves. He estimated going through hundreds of pairs of gloves throughout his career. His fellow firefighters would tease him every chance they got.

In middle school, Rick was always listening to his local fire department respond to calls on his radio scanner. He became a reserve firefighter before he graduated high school. Over the next two decades he would rise through the fire ranks as a firefighter, engineer, and captain.

After the Oklahoma City bombing, Rick's interests were pushed toward USAR after reading an article in a firefighting periodical. The same article featured the disaster search dogs. Later, when the call came down for volunteers for the handler job in my pilot program, Rick put his hand up. He was the exact carte blanche I needed. He took the assignment seriously. He knew his dog's actions could mean the difference between life and death. His pursuit of perfection would take a special dog when it came to canine assignment, but we would cross that bridge when we got to it. For the time being, it was great to have another type-A personality to share a home away from home.

Also joining us for training would be firefighter Randy Gross. Randy was an easygoing guy who was quick to strike up a conversation. Behind his youthful smile was a man who could turn serious in an instant, and he took his job very seriously. Randy got into firefighting first as a volunteer firefighter, following in the footsteps of his father in the El Dorado Hills Fire Department. He eventually became a full-time firefighter a few years later before becoming involved in USAR and my pilot program.

Rob Cima was our third volunteer. Quiet and reserved,

Rob was also a lifelong firefighter who had deployed in response to the Oklahoma City bombing. He had no idea about what was involved in training a search dog, but he'd seen what good dogs could do, so joining the pilot program was an easy call for him to make.

With the Three Rs—Rick, Randy, and Rob—I had a quorum. I let the firefighters know we were doing something that had never been done before. I told them the success of the SDF depended on our success in the pilot program. If we worked together toward our common goal, I had no doubt we would succeed. If we did our own things and let the doubts and unknown get the better of us, we would fail. It was that simple. I also threw them a curveball. I said, "I only expect you to work as hard as I do." They looked at me, a graying, retired sixty-three-year-old, and probably thought, *How hard can it be?*

What they didn't see was that I lived and breathed the SDF pilot program, day in and day out. If I were going to break, it would've happened a long time ago. At this point, my attitude was, show me an obstacle and I'll show you a woman who's made up her mind. The firefighters would need to meet me on that level. We got down to business.

WORD TRAVELS FAST in the firefighter community and your reputation often precedes you. In my case, this was fortunate as my less-than-formidable physical appearance was supplemented by my track record. The firefighters had either been there or read the after-action reports from the Oklahoma City disaster. I had been there, and my three firefighters knew it was to their benefit to listen.

And so, primed and focused, they showed up as the sun rose for their first day of training. I gathered them around to distribute their training equipment. They leaned in, eager to receive the storied tools of the canine disaster search trade. I handed them two bags for collecting dog poop.

"Always have two of these on you," I said. "A wedding, an airport, I don't care. Have two of them."

They stared at me.

I handed them each a leash. "Your leash," I said. "It can be anywhere on you, but have it always. And here is the whistle for controlling the dog when shouting is not appropriate. Your whistle will be around your neck."

They took the equipment glumly, obviously underwhelmed. But I had yet to give them the most critical piece of training equipment. A fantastic training device I'd picked up from my time observing military canine training at Lackland Air Force Base. I handed each firefighter a white bucket. "For now," I said without an ounce of humor. "This is your dog."

Though they probably thought otherwise, this was not a joke. The first lesson of being a handler actually has nothing to do with a dog's movements. The dogs take cues from their handler's movements—*every* movement. Dogs are masters when it comes to interpreting human behavior as they've been by our side for an estimated thirty thousand years. Thus before the handler even touched fur, they would need to learn how and when to move. For example, if they wanted to leave their dog in a down-stay, they had to step off with their right foot; otherwise, the dog would interpret the movement as one where she needs to come along. The handlers needed to learn that the dog watches every subtle movement, interprets it, and reacts. Hence the bucket—a stationary object the handlers could reference as they focused elsewhere. The military does the same thing for new canine handler recruits.

By this time, we had attracted quite an audience. Through the firehouse's windows, a number of other firefighters were watching their buddies, who'd probably bragged about elite search dog training, now get poop-bag decrees and give commands to buckets like lunatics. I'm sure it took them a while to live that down. Rob would admit later he wasn't sure, at first, if I had all my faculties.

I, of course, paid it no mind. Doubts were all too familiar territory. Rick, Rob, and Randy were wondering just what the hell they'd signed up for, but we started working the basics immediately, and I didn't give them a free minute to form any more doubts.

IN TWO WEEKS, we rotated through blocks of instruction on basic obedience, dog behavior, scenting, and the use of voice, human body, and timing for commands. We worked on being a practice "victim"—playing tug-of-war with the reward toy and other skills to make it more fun and better training for the dog. Then we brought in Murphy to let them work with an already trained dog and start understanding a dog's body language.

The firefighters worked incredibly hard. They suffered through hours with me and then had to go immediately into their normal firefighter shifts. Any time we traveled, they had to use personal vacation time. But they completed everything to standard, and I felt that they were ready for the next step. We set a date to head to Sundowners Kennels and get their dogs.

I'd given the firefighters some background on their potential canine partners. I didn't sugarcoat anything. The handlers would know their dog inside and out soon enough anyway. With her penchant for destruction and general mayhem, Ana worried the firefighters. Nobody wanted to deal with that type of energy, especially someone who's never handled a trained dog. Rick Lee wore a particularly concerned look as he heard how Ana had systematically dismantled my living room. He would confess later that his thoughts amounted to, "I hope I don't get *that* dog." Randy shared his sentiments when I described Dusty's similar wild-child behavior. Time would only tell which dog would go where.

———

FEBRUARY 3, 1997, WAS judgment day in Gilroy, California. Time for the rubber to meet the road as the firefighters
received their dogs and actually became a team. First thing
was first; they had to choose their dogs, or rather, let their
dogs choose them with a little help from Pluis.

An early morning fog still hung on the mountains in
the background as the three firefighters stepped out onto
the fifty-foot square of lush green grass portioned off by a
brown wooden fence at Sundowners Kennels. They all
wore sweatshirts of some sort against the winter chill.
They didn't know what to expect. From the corner, Pluis
looked on, quiet and seemingly indifferent, but her mind
was running a mile a minute. When the dogs appeared
she would be watching body language of both canine and
human. The chemistry between dog and handler had to
be spot-on. Under the extreme demands and pressure of
a disaster search, any fissures could grow to cracks and
eventually cave.

The firefighters waited in the empty field, pockets full
of poop bags, fidgeting nervously. No plastic buckets here.
It was time for the real deal—what they'd been training
for. The gate opened and the firefighters got the first
glimpses of their future partners.

First came Ana. She bounded in, head high, prim and
proper, but sped up to the pace of a laser beam. She sniffed
the area, executing precise pivots and turns in her calculated way, then introduced herself to each of the firefighters. Pluis watched. The firefighters greeted the high-energy

princess in turn, wondering if she'd be their future partner. Rick knew this was the infamous pup I'd warned
him about.

Next was Dusty. The auburn girl tore across the field
in a full battle charge, all wild emotion. Her hyperactive
personality matched Ana's, but she had more muscle to
boost her flood of exuberance. Despite her bold show of
force, her confidence was balanced on pillars of sand. It
would take time to overcome her past abuse, and any over-
bearing control by her handler would crumble her confidence. She would need a firm lead to keep her power in
check but in a kind way that only built her up. Dusty
slowed her jet engines to landing speed and tentatively exchanged greetings with the firefighters. Pluis looked on.

Finally came the kind soul. Harley ran in, full steam
ahead. Compared to an average dog, especially one of his
size, Harley was incredibly fast. But compared to his sib-
lings, he was more lumbering. Harley's task-driven personality and big heart demanded a pairing with someone
with an even keel and a quiet but steady compassion.
Harley exchanged greetings with the firefighters and then
was ushered out of the training field.

A thick silence descended on the field with the depar-
ture of the dogs as Pluis made her final considerations. The
firefighters had their own predictions. This would be a
major intersection for their career, one that could affect
the rest of their lives. All three dogs were again let into
the training area. Without ceremony, Pluis doled out the

leashes. Later, she explained her decisions to me. She needed handlers who were the human mirrors of the dogs.

Rick Lee was an intense professional, always seeking perfection. Pluis knew there was one dog that could take that intensity and match it. She handed Rick Ana's leash. For all his fretting, he should've known it was coming.

Randy Gross was laid-back but still had a calculated focus when the situation called for it. He'd raised daughters and knew how to hold an edge, but could be gentle about applying it. Pluis handed him Dusty's leash.

Rob Cima was pragmatic and disciplined, but he knew how to quietly connect with teammates, when to push, and when to back off. He received Harley's leash. He was tough enough to handle Harley's extra muscle, and his introspective personality would meld perfectly with our special boy's temperament.

"Now," Pluis announced with an air of suspense, "we may switch."

And with that, the new teams began their training together. They would not switch.

TRAINING BECAME FAST and furious. We'd start at Sundowners Kennels early in the morning and work until noon. I would've kept going straight through until the sun set, but firefighters need to eat. So for an hour, the dogs would take a siesta in their crates and the handlers and trainers would take lunch in a nearby diner. We'd talk lessons learned from the morning's session and corrections to be made.

By the third day, the chemistry between the dogs and their new trainers was palpable. Instead of looking for Pluis, the dogs were looking for the firefighters. The new teams would be finishing each other's sentences in no time (metaphorically, of course). I knew there would be more trials to come before they faced FEMA certification, but the critical element for success was there. I could see it in the dogs' eyes when they looked at their handlers— Ana to Rick, Dusty to Randy, and Harley to Rob. It was a look that said, without question, you are the one.

Twelve

ALL TOGETHER NOW

We returned to Sacramento by the end of February 1997. It would be the final push before I let the birds fly from the nest. We launched into the full gauntlet of training, holding nothing back. We restarted the fundamentals with obedience, but with everything kicked up a notch. The firefighters weren't dealing with plastic buckets anymore, beside them was the partner who'd accompany them into the breach. We enjoyed ourselves, but everyone understood how serious this training was.

We hit the obstacles harder and faster, envisioning not the manicured agility course, but the daunting rubble pile it represented. When it came to searching, we pulled out all the stops. We went into mad-scientist mode, renting a

Hollywood smoke machine to watch how airborne scents would spread over rubble piles. We pumped small structures full of smoke until the tiny tendrils spilled out minute cracks. The scents did not always behave as we expected, sometimes showing up in strange places, places that seemed to defy logic. It hammered home the lesson that the dogs could pick up scent anywhere and needed to be taken seriously every time they alerted. Slowly but surely, the firefighters learned to trust their dogs.

OF COURSE TRAINING was not without its setbacks when it came to the dogs. These are the prodigal sons and daughters of the dog world, not the teacher's pets. Even though they'd been trained well, the dogs still had a wild side that would never leave them. It helped them keep their edge when it came to searching, but also made for some very amusing incidents.

Once, for example, Ana got the urge for a run while Rick had her secured at the firehouse. Calling upon some of her old escape tricks, she timed a few firefighters going out of the station's gate and slipped out unnoticed. She darted across the street and into a walking trail system that bordered the station. Then she went exploring. While Rick casually went about his business, ignorant of the jailbreak, Ana was miles away, chasing ducks and frolicking in the springtime wildflowers. Eventually, she arrived at a manicured park, filled with people enjoying the sunshine.

Soon, Rick's phone was inundated with messages. He saw the emergency dispatch number flash on his screen and knew something was up. Then he listened to a strange voicemail about a firedog on the loose. Thinking Ana was still secured at the station, he was ready to dismiss the message when dispatch described Ana to a T. Rick remembered her wild history and the truth set in. He raced back to collect his delinquent search dog. When he arrived at the park, Ana was sitting like a perfect angel next to a family at a picnic bench. She greeted Rick happily.

"Your dog is so well behaved!" one of the family said with glee. "We've been feeding her cheese and pancakes all morning!"

Rick smiled but could feel a headache setting in. Ana and most working dogs are on a strictly regulated diet and any changes, especially of the "junk food" variety, would mean an upset stomach and everything that comes with it. Good thing I'd trained him to have spare poop bags on hand!

DUSTY DIDN'T HAVE Ana's sweet tooth, but her weakness was squirrels on the loose. That toy drive she exhibited out on the rubble pile was an instinct based on actual prey drive, after all. Chasing squirrels was probably so far embedded into Dusty girl's DNA that no amount of training would keep it at bay. It could only be tempered by a leash . . . which, sometimes, Randy forgot.

Once, Dusty and Randy had been putting on a demonstration for local fire departments about the capabilities of search dogs. Dusty did a demo search and some agility work and left the audience amazed, as was expected. During a break from the action, Randy walked Dusty to a nearby park to relax. With the park more or less empty, he let Dusty off her leash. Suddenly, at the far corner of the park was a flurry of scampering and the brown flash of a bushy tail. Nature took its course. Randy screamed, "NO!" but it did no good. The dog whose training and discipline he'd just raved about to an audience now tore across the field, hell-bent for leather and ignoring any and every command except the instinctual call of the hunt. The chase was on.

When Randy thought things couldn't get any worse, from behind a picnic bench walked a small child. He was walking slowly, head down, and completely oblivious to the pursuit unfolding in the park field next to him. He was also walking right into the path of Dusty's charge.

Dusty did not slow. Her entire world was the squirrel and everything else was a trivial detail. A brick wall would not have stopped her, so a small child wouldn't even be cause for pause.

Randy screamed and yelled but it was too late. The collision was inevitable. Dusty hit the kid with the force of a missile. The kid was thrown off his feet like a rag doll and completed a somersault and a half before slamming back into the earth. The child's mother appeared, screaming her own opinions of Dusty, and they weren't quite the same as the audience's at the demonstration. Now Randy had to worry about Pluis and me murdering him for forgetting a leash, and a family who was about to sue him for all he was worth.

Randy checked the child out and everyone calmed down. Having lost the squirrel, Dusty transformed back from a wolf to a trained working dog, and made a gleeful appearance to greet the child. She couldn't get everywhere with her good looks and charm, but she could get pretty damn far, and they certainly helped quell the storm in this case. It was determined the kid had cracked his collarbone, and Randy offered to cover any medical expenses. The family took pity on the firefighter and forgave Dusty for her transgression. Everybody left the incident a little wiser. Randy might've avoided repercussions from the family, but I did not show him mercy. Needless to say, he didn't forget the leash again.

AS TRAINING PROGRESSED, the dogs got stronger. Each day, they seemed to move faster, more smoothly, and to want more when we finished. One more run through the obstacles; one more search; one more chance to get their toy reward. Everything else—how hot it was, how much food they ate, the time of day—fell away.

The firefighters did great, too, giving maximum effort during training and then slaving away studying doctrine and lessons learned after hours. They were burning the

candle at both ends and a little bit in the middle because
they had to attend to their normal firefighter and family
duties in addition to the dogs. When our time finally came
to a close two months later, they were more than ready to
collapse on the couch (I might've broken a sweat, too).
Rick, Rob, and Randy had exceeded my expectations.
They knew their job. The dogs were ready, too. Ana was
spot on, she just needed a little slowing down. Dusty
brimmed with confidence, her alerting just needed to be
a little more precise. Harley had grown to love obstacles.
He was a little rough around the edges and his obedience
needed constant maintenance, but overall he was an incredible dog—a searching machine. I knew it wouldn't be
long before they all could take on FEMA certification and
become deployment ready.

The Search Dog Foundation itself, on the other hand,
gave me pause. Once the three teams passed their FEMA
certification, I could technically call the SDF pilot program a success. But I wasn't planning on stopping there.
Not for a second. In terms of employees, SDF was still a
one-woman-band; it was only the dedication of a few loyal
volunteers that was keeping us running. While I'd been
training the firefighters, I'd been neglecting some of the
organizational requirements for the nonprofit. We were
standing on shaky legs financially. What I didn't know was
that for all our success in the field, we were losing ground
on the budget side of the equation, and edging closer to
going off a cliff.

Thirteen

OUR NEW HOME IS THE CITY DUMP

The test was coming. The FEMA Canine SAR Certification test would eventually merge into a single exam, but in 1997, there were two separate tests. Basic certification—two victims across two rubble piles in under fifteen minutes—allowed the qualifier to respond to local disasters. Advanced certification—six victims across three rubble piles in under forty minutes—allowed a team to deploy nationally and internationally. My goal had always been to help our nation, so none of our teams would settle for only Basic certification. And although the FEMA Advanced certification was needed to respond to disasters, the certifications themselves weren't the desired end state. We needed teams who were at their best at actual disasters, where stress would be through the roof and there would no doubt be behavioral factors nobody could predict.

THERE WERE OTHER SAR canine groups that wanted to push their teams through as fast as possible. They'd show up with only half-baked training experience. Maybe their dogs would pass, maybe not. To the firefighters, this was unacceptable. They lived by a mantra: at the moment of truth, you will not rise to the level of your expectations, you will fall to the level of your training. Before they even thought about taking the FEMA certification tests, the Three Rs, and thus the SDF, wanted teams that were, without question, ready for deployment. Rick, Rob, and Randy knew they had first-class search dogs. They took it personally that they were the anchors on their team and, to the delight of the dogs, trained like hell to get themselves up to speed.

Ironically, one of the greatest obstacles in their training path was a lack of obstacles. All living in the Sacramento area, the Three Rs could easily coordinate their fire department schedules, and of course the dogs always wanted to work. But you can't exactly have a rubble pile on standby. There's no way to just throw together a few tons of collapsed concrete or inflate a pile of twisted steel. For this reason, one area of training we really hadn't been able to cover was searching on a *real* rubble pile. All the hours on obstacles and agility courses wouldn't amount to much if the dogs couldn't perform on the real course.

The firefighters knew they needed to get out on rubble, so they made it happen. They descended on recycling centers and city dumps and talked attendants into letting them run the dogs over trash piles and lumber stacks. The firefighters would come home happy, but smelling like trash. They befriended demolition crews around the Sacramento area. At first, these crews worried about liability— destroyed buildings are dangerous places, after all—but eventually the crews would end for the day and hand it over to the search teams with one request: "Just make sure we don't find any bodies here in the morning."

The dogs ate up the new time on rubble and refined their skills, so the firefighters increased the intensity. They tried everything. Training under time limits. Training cold searches without prior knowledge—one would organize the rubble pile location and the buried victims, and the others would show up last minute and start searching immediately, just like an emergency deployment. Sometimes they wouldn't even have victims because more often than not, that is what happens in a real disaster. The dogs had to get used to searching and searching with no live finds.

The teams trained at night, in low light with flashlights and chemical glow lights, experimenting with different tools and techniques with the dogs. They brought in a field trials expert to teach them the nuances of retrieval work. They experimented with different reward toys. For Ana and Dusty, the toy of choice was a section of old fire hose that Rick and Randy sewed together stuffed with socks. Harley preferred something softer and fuzzy. Beanie Babies became his favorite, so Rob came to tote pocketfuls of bright and smiley stuffed animals. He had to bear the heckling from the other handlers of course, but if it helped his dog, Rob didn't care; he would've happily juggled the toys while singing falsetto.

The teams came up with new places to test their dogs. They searched the ball pits in funhouses. They even searched the Piedmont jailhouse, abandoned before it was to be demolished, in the dead of night. The jail was underground so it had absolutely no ambient light. Talk about creepy.

The teams approached each training session like they would deploy the next day. When the firefighters spoke of their training, they always held that they needed to conduct each search like it was for a member of their own family. When it came down to it, one day they *would* be searching for someone's family member.

The dogs flourished. They loved searching, and now that they had a positive environment, a stable home, and a loving owner, they were thriving. It didn't take long for the media to catch wind of a group of firefighters who were lingering around demolished buildings with dogs that ran over rubble like saving angels. One evening a news crew joined the firefighters as they searched a freshly demolished mall complex. When the reporter cornered the teams and started asking questions, a normally reticent Rob Cima stepped up to the microphone with Harley by his side.

"We train because we have one shot at this, and you don't want to miss," he said. "And these dogs don't miss."

It was a philosophy the teams took to heart. If the day came, they would be ready. Rick might just need a few extra pairs of gloves.

GLOVES OR NOT, in May 1997, Rick Lee thought Ana was ready for her FEMA Basic Disaster Canine SAR Certification. She had been training for only seven months, and together with Rick for only four months. Certifying now would be the equivalent of going from peewee league to the pros in less than a year. It was unheard of. Anyone who had not seen Ana search dismissed it as a fantasy. Even those close to the team had their reservations. But Rick trusted Ana. She checked every box on every search without fail.

On the morning of May 18, Rick opened Ana's crate at a rubble pile of crushed concrete near Sacramento. An ever-tranquil Ana did a few concise stretches and looked to Rick with the electric gleam that let him know she was ready to go to work, and God help any soul that stood in her way. Before them were three elevated platforms, an agility course, and two sprawling rubble piles of concrete slabs, shattered wood, and twisted pipes. Multiple evaluators stood around the course, clipboards ready.

Ana first went through basic obedience commands, a snooze fest for her. Then came a direction and control test, where she would ascend one of the three elevated platforms, wait for a command from Rick, and follow a specified pattern around and to the next platform, about twenty-five yards away. Ana had no problems here either, finishing in just over one minute. Then it was on to the agility course. Ana had to complete four mandatory obstacles—ladder, elevated plank, tunnel, and unstable surface—and then one other handler's choice obstacle within five minutes, all while staying under control, and obeying any directions by the handler. A cakewalk.

Then it was really show time: the rubble pile search. Ana needed to find two victims buried in multiple rubble piles in under fifteen minutes. Rick led her to the starting point, went through his pre-search checklist, and unleashed Ana.

"Search!" he commanded.

Ana straight-lined toward an alcove on the rubble pile and immediately started her alert bark. The evaluators exchanged glances. She'd found the first victim so fast Rick had tripped and fell trying to keep up with her. Ana continued her bark alert and Rick picked himself up and made his way over to "call" the find—officially confirming for the evaluators that a dog had found a live victim. In a real disaster, this would be where the handler radios for the rescue squad and rewards the dog.

One down, one to go. Rick gave Ana a quick once-over to check for injuries and then loosed her again.

No hesitation or searching patterns. Again, Ana went almost directly to a second spot on the rubble and started her alert bark. Second victim found. The elapsed time was under five minutes. Nobody knew what to make of it because nobody had ever seen anything like it.

Rick and Ana exited the pile. Ana got her tug toy reward and shook it triumphantly, then jumped in a nearby kiddy pool to celebrate. Everyone looked on in a kind of awestruck reverence. This dog was incredible. Rick had heard an earlier comment from a bystander that because Ana was finding victims so fast the evaluators thought she'd cheated somehow.

The vilification of the SDF program hadn't diminished with our successes. Unfortunately, it had only spread to those working with me. Everyone from the trainers to the firefighters heard the doubts and naysayers at every turn. A large number of so-called professionals didn't think firefighters should be allowed to be handlers. Rick, Rob, and Randy had to confront such biases at what seemed like every turn. At one training event, Rick was volunteering as a "victim" for other dogs when a pair of civilian judges, unaware he was "buried" beneath them, came over and spent a good few minutes badmouthing the firefighters. At other training events, some evaluators would purposely

put extra safety judges on the rubble pile to try to con-
fuse SDF dogs.

But Rick wasn't worried about gossip. He'd heard all
the skepticism before and ignored the whispers. Ana could
do it all again in a blink of an eye, and anyone who watched
her search would agree, regardless of their bias. She'd completed every task without flaw; the evaluators really had
no choice but to certify her. By the end of the day, we
got the official word. Ana was certified.

Rick and I knelt and praised Ana, who was still ec-
statically floundering in her princess pool. Just one year
ago an unadoptable house pet and a rejected assistance dog
with no future, this Golden girl was now certified to search
out trapped humans anywhere in California. She had exceeded all expectations and defied all the odds. Her success was exceptional and proved our program could work.
I still had 167 teams to go to reach my internal goal, but
suddenly it didn't seem like just a fleeting daydream.

Four months later, Dusty and Randy Gross would try
for their FEMA Basic certification. Prior to the test, however, there was a problem. Dusty, probably stemming
from her troubled past, was ultra-sensitive to the mood
around her. As Randy's anxiousness for the test grew,
Dusty sensed the change and grew uneasy. Doubts about
the situation began to creep in. Was it something she'd
done? When the dogs aren't searching, they are usually
kept in crates. They learn that their crate, wherever it lies,
is their safe place. For a dog that always wants to work, it

is the symbol that, for now, their work is done and they can relax. For this reason, I was very strict about crating dogs. But suddenly for Dusty, the tension in the air made the crate too small. Something was wrong and she didn't know what. Her anxiety begat more anxiety. She wouldn't lie down. She paced in her crate, mewing and whining, despite Randy's reassurances. It was a problem. Not only was she getting more upset, she was burning herself out before they'd even started. By the time they hit the rubble pile, she'd already be spent. Randy had to do something. Though totally against my instructions, Randy relied on his instincts with Dusty. He'd been the one putting in hundreds of hours, paw-in-hand with Dusty and knew exactly what his nervous partner needed. He pulled Dusty out of her crate, and sat her in his lap. Until they were ready to start the test, he spoke soothing words to her and stroked her head. It worked. Dusty calmed and settled back into her trained mindset. When their number was called to search, Dusty was ready. She tore through the course and achieved her certification. Both she and Ana would receive their FEMA Advanced certifications within the next few months.

Harley, steady and relentless in his searching, would, with Rob Cima, achieve his FEMA Basic certification around the same time Ana and Dusty were testing for Advanced. Compared to his adopted sisters, Harley was a bit slower, but he was almost a full year faster than 99 percent of other search dogs at the time.

When it came time for Harley's Advanced certification test a few months later, things were going smoothly and Rob was confident with his performance. I watched Harley check off his task list, finding five victims in the pile and giving strong bark alerts. Rob thought that would be it, but then Harley alerted again on a woodpile at the corner of the rubble. Rob knew there could be up to six victims, but saw no way they could hide somebody in a place like that. He didn't know why Harley was alerting, but thought it was probably nothing. He hesitated to call it because calling a false alert is an automatic failure. I watched from the sidelines. Harley continued to bark, and Rob continued to hesitate. I felt my blood start to boil. Finally, he did the right thing and called it. Of course, out pops a sixth victim from the woodpile. Harley had passed. Rob, well, he needed a piece of my mind. I approached him—he probably thought I was going to congratulate him—and let him have it. "What the hell were you thinking?" I demanded. "You didn't trust your dog!"

Rob learned from his mistake, but, more important, Harley was Advanced certified. Three teams had entered the pilot program, three had graduated, and now all three were certified to respond to disasters across the nation. Depending on which data point you consider, we'd reduced training time by almost two-thirds. We'd shaved years off the process and our dogs were top-notch. The SDF was moving. Onward and upward.

Fourteen

PART-TIME MEANS FULL-TIME

The SDF's first office would eventually be turned into a storage closet. It was a tiny little cell on the first floor of a small office building in Ojai, California, a shared space with another local nonprofit that organized music festivals. Crammed in next to me was Debra Tosch, only slightly taller than myself, who had honey-wheat hair and always seemed to be smiling. Debra had responded to an ad I'd placed in the local paper, requesting volunteers. Like me, she made up for any lack of experience (and physical stature) with pure willpower. When she started in 1996, I didn't know how large a role she would eventually play in the success of the foundation. But for the time being, we were two sardines, jammed in a tiny can. At least the price was right for the small office—$125 a month. You can't get a parking spot in Southern California for that price now.

Debra was living in an RV and studying for her CPA exam, having gone to school and set her sights on becoming an accountant. Her help and her financial advice was invaluable for the foundation. She was a formidable second-in-command and I was offloading more and more tasks onto her as she thrived in both the numbers and the canine-related business. I needed her full-time, but could only pay her part-time. Graciously, she accepted a part-time, minimum wage salary ($8.00 an hour at the time) and volunteered the rest of her time. She kept track of her hours on notecards, which quickly filled up and spilled over onto a yellow legal pad, but Debra didn't complain once.

What Debra probably saw better than I or any of the volunteers was that the foundation itself was struggling financially. We had purpose, but even the most noble of organizations require the fundamentals for survival— workspace, employees, and money. As much as I hated it, funding is the lifeblood of a nonprofit. The SDF was no different. We needed more dogs, and each dog required more vet care, food, boarding, and training. All of these cost money. The speed of the pilot program showed we could cut required funds for producing a search dog down by more than one-third, but on the scale I wished to achieve, it still needed a massive amount of fundraising.

The initial outburst of support from my close friends and associates was drying up quickly. Our only revenue streams were selling watermelons and SDF pencils for small donations at nearby bake sales. We would run rattlesnake–avoidance clinics for local pets, where the proceeds benefited the foundation. These got local press attention, but it didn't amount to much. I found myself reaching for my own checkbook more and more often.

I didn't stop to worry about it—there was no time. I would face the consequences later.

And face them I would.

Fifteen

THE SHERMANATOR AND STRETCH ARMSTRONG

While Ana, Dusty, and Harley checked off FEMA certifications, one other area we were having more and more success with was finding dogs. As word spread of what we were trying to do, I started to get volunteers checking more shelters outside of Ojai in places like Santa Barbara and San Diego. Because of our Foreign Legion, take-all-comers policy, we started to acquire a colorful cast of characters.

Sherman was a dark Chocolate Labrador with eyebrows that turned upward like he was permanently asking a question. He was less than a year old but already built like the main battle tank that shared his name. His adopting family became overwhelmed with his brute strength and almost-scary power. In their defense, the Russian powerlifting team probably would've been overwhelmed by his strength. The eight-foot fence that surrounded the backyard of Sherman's prep home before he came to the SDF was no match. He would throw his huge frame against the fence so hard it shook and get his front paws over the top. Then, with the pure muscle of a gymnast doing a pull-up, he'd get himself over and out into the world. The family knew there would be no way they could handle this dog as a full-grown adult. Before Sherman could be surrendered to the shelter, he came to the attention of an SDF volunteer who evaluated potential search dog candidates. She saw instincts in Sherman that mirrored what was needed in a search dog: he would bark alert on a toy; he would chase that toy ceaselessly; he had the strength and endurance to continue the chase all day. I welcomed him into the SDF with open arms. No shelter for the Shermanator; he had a new career. In late 1997, the giant pup was crammed into the car and transported to Sundowners Kennels to begin his tutelage under Pluis.

BILLY WAS A Black Labrador with soft, knowing eyes that gave the impression that, if the pup could talk, you'd have a very nice conversation together. Billy was the antithesis of Sherman. He didn't look like what you would think of as an athlete dog. When he would sit down, his shoulders would round, and his neck would slump. Even early in his life, the fur around his mouth had a sprinkling of white, like he'd just eaten a powdered donut. At a glance, Billy would easily be mistaken for a lazy couch dog. On the contrary, his small and wiry frame made Billy quick and agile on any terrain, and he had a hell of a prey drive. A local woman rescued Billy from a shelter in Apple Valley, California. Billy's energy and toy-obsessed behavior quickly became too much for the woman to handle, but she got word to one of our SDF volunteers, who then evaluated the dog. Thus, Billy came to live with me in Ojai.

I saw Billy's potential, but didn't realize the full extent of his drive until one day, John was throwing a toy ball for him in the backyard. On one throw, the ball took a bad bounce and skipped through our wrought iron fence. Before John could move, Billy charged the fence. As he neared the fence, he didn't slow down. Instead, he wriggled through a gap so small he yelped when it came time to get his hips through, but he stretched out as thin as he could and that dog made it. And then he got the ball! No need to question his drive after that. I knew Billy would make a great candidate, and I knew Pluis could harness his drive and "Stretch Armstrong" abilities to make him a first-class search dog.

ZACK WAS A Chocolate Lab puppy who never grew out of being a puppy. He had a lean but angled frame like a sharp arrow and a diving board of a tongue. From the moment he was born through his fourteen years, Zack maintained the same inexhaustible energy level. Unlike other dogs, Zack did not mellow with age. He might've had solar panels hidden on his slender back because his switch was always on and his battery never ran dry. Zack was a lot to handle, but his owner, firefighter Jeff Place, was prepared and knew this was his future partner. When Jeff was looking through the litter of puppies, Zack bounded out, grabbed the keys to Jeff's truck in his mouth, and started tromping over to the vehicle like, *C'mon, let's go!*

Jeff was not only a firefighter but also an animal rescuer: he dedicated his time to caring for abandoned and abused dogs in the San Francisco Bay Area shelters around where he lived. He'd already wanted to be a search dog handler, but lacked the local support of his fire department. Undeterred, Jeff began working with his little perpetual motor Zack as soon as he adopted the puppy. He began putting himself through the courses necessary to be a canine handler on his own dime and his own time. I was impressed with Jeff's dedication, but a little worried. When a handler raises a puppy, the dog is usually not able to reach its potential as a search dog. It would be like trying to be a drill sergeant for your own children—on some level, you'd probably overlook their weaknesses. But Jeff was determined.

With Sherman and Billy already on deck, and Ana, Dusty, and Harley just a few months beyond graduation, the SDF did not have the funds to send Zack through Pluis's training. Again, Jeff refused to give up. He paid himself. I had to admire his persistence, and as long as he met the standards, I wasn't going to stand in his way. I was honored to have Jeff on the team, and thought his driven Lab would be a perfect fit. Zack, teeming with endless puppy enthusiasm, followed Sherman and Billy to Sundowners Kennels for training.

IN THE FALL of 1997, Sherman and Billy and Zack started their course with Pluis. This was round two of the Search Dog Foundation. We now knew it was possible, but was it replicable? Sherman and Billy and Zack brought their own unique set of strengths and weaknesses. Pluis began their training to see if they would be able to follow in the paw prints of their predecessors.

Sherman's only issue in training was stopping. Pluis had to accumulate a lot of bruises in order to get Sherman to control himself after he got a head of steam and attacked an obstacle. She also had to be cautious about what was in Sherman's path; an unanchored obstacle would be smashed to pieces because Sherman had no fear of consequences. Once Sherman was throttled down a tad, he excelled. Four stars in all training phases.

Billy's "Stretch Armstrong" body didn't smash things like Sherman's hulking frame. He had tremendous drive but was much softer in terms of training. He was a very thoughtful dog and he loved to be correct. If, in a training iteration, he did not succeed, he would take it very hard. Pluis had to approach him much like she did with Dusty in the pilot program, gentle but firm. As long as she walked the line, Billy did not dwell on his defeats. Being a master, Pluis kept Billy on an even keel and soon he was excelling right next to Sherman.

Zack did not struggle with the individual training but when it came time to go back to his firefighter, Jeff Place, things became a little more difficult. Even with Jeff aware of overcompensating for the dog, Zack was such an intelligent creature that he knew exactly how to play his handler when he didn't want to do something. Pluis had a delightful time watching Zack push boundaries. At first, Zack would refuse to complete a task and Jeff would make excuses for his dear pup, just like a parent would do for his child. Then Pluis would step in as the handler and Zack would perform the task correctly. It took a little time, but eventually Jeff learned to keep Zack in line and the pair improved more and more. It was soon clear to everyone Zack would be an excellent search dog. In early 1998, all three dogs were paired with handlers and set for graduation.

SHERMAN WENT HOME with his handler, firefighter Steve Swaney, for the first time. The long drive back to Steve's home near San Diego allowed the big Lab to settle in and get some well-deserved rest. Steve had a young daughter strapped into a car seat next to Sherman, and the two became fast friends. An onlooker might be dubious about pairing such a massive dog with the father of a toddler, but anyone who knew Sherman would not hesitate—the big guy was the gentlest giant in the world. As Steve went to get burgers at a pit stop along the drive home, Sherman just wanted to stay in the car with the rest of his new family. When Steve returned, Sherman was snuggled up asleep next to his daughter, content as could be.

Sherman was immediately dropped into the training pipeline with his handler. Sherman was a bull in a china shop, except the whole world was his china shop. At his El Cajon firehouse, he wasn't satisfied with the miniature firehouse chew toys, and instead opted for the super size, pulling an entire fire hose across the yard. His strength became legendary. When other handlers watched after Sherman, they first had to review a long checklist of dos and don'ts—not for Sherman, but rather for their own safety.

Once, Debra helped out as a "buried victim" at one of Sherman's training searches. She held his reward toy tightly in her hand. "Make him work for it," Steve had told her. So she clutched it close to her body and only had a short wait before Sherman's deep baritone bark shook her hiding spot. Steve called the find, and Debra held out the reward tug toy. The next thing she knew she was flying through the air. Sherman had snatched the toy and was dragging Debra across the entire training site like a fish on a line.

Sherman was unstoppable on a search. When he was on the rubble pile, nothing else in the world existed. During one mock search, Sherman was so focused on finding the buried victim, he ran headlong into a plate glass window blocking his way. Instead of being stymied, Sherman re-cocked and rammed the plate glass window again. Before any of the shocked onlookers could stop him, Sherman charged a third time. The still-shaking glass held, but finally Sherman got the idea and took the easier route around the window and found the victim.

Going into the FEMA certification tests, Steve wasn't even nervous. Sherman was unshakeable. In the fifteen minutes they were allotted for their FEMA Basic certification, Sherman found the victim in less than four minutes. Some dogs have drive but this dog was *driven*. In February 1999, Sherman rumbled into his FEMA Advanced certification and left victorious. He was the first to do so since our pilot program.

Seeing the enormous progress the dogs were making in their training, we weren't exactly on the edge of our seats waiting for this milestone, but it was nice to finally get confirmation that we could successfully replicate the training. The validation of our model was heartening and fantastic for the morale of our foundation, but there were still so many dogs to rescue, and many were promising candidates.

Sixteen

DUKE AND THE
VELCRO DOG

n 1998, I found a dog who wagged his long tail so hard it split open. Even that didn't stop him from wagging, so the wound never healed. Bandages were no match. Eventually, the untenable tail had to be partially amputated to avoid infection. Even afterward, the dog still had a formidable tail. And it continued to wag. This was Duke. At eighty-five pounds, this massive Chocolate Lab was nearly as big as Debra Tosch, so of course I picked her as Duke's caretaker while we waited for an opening at Pluis's kennel.

Duke was a rejected hunting dog. Plenty of drive and heart, but as a former caretaker put it, "he only has two brain cells and they have yet to meet." True, Duke had a bit more brawn than brain, but this dog loved to work.

Nothing made his tail wag harder. I knew he would make a fantastic search dog based on sheer willpower alone. Until he started his training, though, Debra had her hands full. She would get waterskiing lessons every time she took him for a "walk" as he dragged her down the bike path near the SDF office.

One night after Duke was in bed in his crate, Debra was awakened by a large *thump*. It sounded like someone breaking into her home. Debra thought fast. *Were the dogs ok? Should she call the police?* She decided to take a peek. When the lights came on, the only vagrant she saw was Duke, an *uh-oh* look on his face, with a tennis ball he'd smuggled into his crate now stuffed in his mouth. He'd been playing with the contraband ball after lights-out like a kid reading comics under the covers past bedtime.

As with many of these search dogs, Duke needed constant stimulation and would make trouble if he felt bored. Once, he snuck into one of our unoccupied office rooms and chewed up a power cord. A power cord that was plugged in. Fortunately, he was unharmed, but it scared the hell out of us. We let out a collective sigh of relief when Duke left to start his training with Pluis. There was no doubt he'd make a phenomenal search dog; we just didn't know how they'd keep him under control without assigning an entire fire brigade as handlers.

———

MANNY NEARLY PUT me in the nuthouse. He was a handsome male Border Collie whose coloring evoked the image of a divine chocolate-caramel-vanilla dessert dish. He was an artist's rendition of the breed: a bright white coat, a symmetrical complement of onyx, and small highlights of bronze. Manny came from an impeccable lineage of show dogs, but the intelligent Collie's impressive pedigree almost became his downfall.

Pedigree is registered with the American Kennel Club and displays things like breed, owner, and the dog's lineage. It follows a show dog much like the title of a car and is a very important piece of documentation as it essentially proves the dog's potential in the show ring. When a dispute arose between the breeder and Manny's potential buyer, the breeder refused to provide the pedigree. Without it, Manny amounted to nothing more than a mutt, worthless in the show ring. He was surrendered to a Border Collie rescue.

The SDF, on the other hand, was happy to have him. We couldn't care less about a dog's background or lineage. If you can search, then we don't ask questions. One of our dedicated volunteers caught wind of Manny and evaluated him. Manny tested very well and soon joined me in my home. That's where he started driving me crazy.

It was my first experience with a Border Collie, and for anyone who's owned one before, they have some very maddening characteristics. They are known as Velcro dogs because wherever you go, they are right by your side, stuck to you like Velcro. Manny followed me everywhere.

Kitchen? Manny was there. Bedroom? Manny was there. Bathroom? Manny was right by my side. *My God,* I thought, *can't you take a break and go lay down for a few minutes?* Manny took no breaks.

Border Collies are also herding dogs. They were originally bred to herd livestock, and Manny still had a full dose of the instinct. With no sheep to herd in my house, Manny made his own—out of my Labs. Murphy, normally the officer-in-charge, now found herself demoted as Manny organized her and the other two Black Labs I had at the time into a "herd" and marched them around the house, nipping at their feet when they weren't moving fast enough, corralling and hustling them wherever he saw fit. The herd and I were ready for a break.

Around that same time, a civilian named Ron Weckbacher approached me about becoming an SDF handler. He was willing to put himself through all the necessary EMS and FEMA classes to get to the same level as our firefighters, and pay for a dog's training in its entirety. I couldn't fault his dedication, and, as fragile as the SDF's financial situation was at the time, I couldn't argue with his plan. So I let Ron take Manny for the week to see if he could handle this Velcro dog for a short period of time. Ron and Manny bonded almost instantly. I was glad to get some peace and quiet, but even happier because I knew Manny would make a great search dog and Ron would make a great handler. Not much later, Manny was at Sundowners doing his best to herd Pluis and her other dogs into line.

Seventeen

THE DRAMA QUEEN AND THE GUNSHOT SURVIVOR

On a back road near a highway in eastern Memphis, Tennessee, from somewhere out of the overgrown thickets of wilderness, perhaps north from the dense forests that lined the Mississippi River, or east from the marshland and backwoods along the Wolf River, limped a young Black Labrador. She was only a few years old, but probably wouldn't live more than a few more days. She was cold and hungry and her side was riddled with buckshot.

But fate and the kindness of a stranger were on her side. The stranger also happened to be veterinarian Lauren Wiltshire, DVM, who had a practice in Memphis. Dr. Wiltshire noticed the Lab running free with no identification and looking injured. The Lab was keeping a good pace despite the injury, and it wasn't until Dr. Wiltshire scooped her up that she realized the extent of the poor dog's trauma. She brought the Lab back to her clinic, removed the buckshot and cleaned out the infection, and gave the dog a name. That's how Lola came to be rescued.

True to her survivor's nature, Lola recovered quickly from her injuries. It wasn't long before she was bouncing off the walls. She loved running and swimming in a local pond. She would constantly be pressing Dr. Wiltshire to throw sticks. The vet didn't quite realize how much Lola obsessed about the stick-chasing game until she threw one a little too far into the pond. Before Lola could make it out to make the retrieval, the stick waterlogged and sank. Lola dove right after the stick, picked it off the bottom of the pond, and returned to shore for another throw. The incident triggered a memory of an article Dr. Wiltshire had read about a little organization looking for rescue dogs with high toy drive. A short time later, I received a call from the good vet.

Lola presented another issue. She was the first dog SDF had located outside of California. How were we supposed to get her here? Any type of shipping would be too dangerous for the dog. My husband, John, was volun-told to lead the mission to bring Lola back.

Once back in California, Lola tested great and seemed ready to start a new career. Soon she was joining the other dogs at Sundowners Kennels to train with Pluis.

THE EASIEST CANDIDATES to come by were gifts from my aging Black Lab, Murphy. By the end of 1997, Murphy had retired from active duty searching, but she was still very capable, and helped coach the new handlers. Any time they needed to see a demonstration done right, I called in Murphy. And she was pregnant. Two months later, she gave us seven wonderful Black Lab pups. As it turned out, two of the pups were prime candidates to become search dogs.

Jefferson, named after the founding father, was a pup whose abilities I had little doubt in from day one. He exuded a confidence that couldn't be taught. He obviously knew where he'd come from and wasn't afraid to show it. He'd inherited Murphy's physical prowess as well, and would no doubt be a handful for his future handler.

Then there was Abby. The only female of the litter, she was named after Abigail Adams. Abby got a full dose of Mother Murphy's talent when it came to search drive. A child prodigy, she had the same confidence as her brother Jefferson. The difference was that where Jeff channeled the talent into cockiness, Abby channeled it into a melodrama of sorts. Like a starlet who only considered starring roles, potential handlers had to earn her respect before she'd work with them. If they didn't know exactly what they were doing or exhibit a commanding enough presence, Abby would take on an offended air. I've never seen a dog pout like she did. Pluis called her a "sulking bitch," and she did not mean it in the canine sense.

Abby also had mercurial relationships with other dogs. Her brother Jefferson was fine, and she became fast friends with Duke and Manny. Billy, the older Black Lab, on the other hand, didn't make the cut. He and Abby would never exactly fight, but rather have constant doggy arguments. Lucky for everyone, Abby joined her buddy Duke as a kennelmate at Sundowners Kennels to see if Pluis could work through Abby's inner teenager.

DEBRA TOSCH APPROACHED me one day in the office, her usual grin a touch more serious, like she was struggling with something. With mild embarrassment, she laid out her plans. The long hours and nonexistent pay and out of control dogs had, miraculously, only made her love of the foundation and its mission grow. She'd decided to forgo taking her CPA exam and become a handler.

I was a little surprised, to say the least. This was a major life decision. She would be giving up a stable career with a sizeable salary for a difficult and dangerous job that paid pennies. She was not a firefighter and would have to take on numerous courses and special training in order to be admitted onto a FEMA task force. But I also knew Debra. She had a spirit that loomed like a giant beyond her small frame. Anything she set her mind to, she could do. Then she dropped a bomb on me.

"I have a German Shepherd," she said. "And I'd like to try wilderness search with him."

Wilderness search? I couldn't believe what I was hearing. She wanted to drop into the quagmire of an SAR group outside of the SDF? All the wasted energy, the stonewalling, the passive-aggressive treatment and flak I'd taken from those groups came rushing back to me. At the time, the rest of the search dog community almost automatically shunned the SDF and anyone associated. And now here was my loyal lieutenant, poised to make the same mistakes I had.

I don't remember exactly what happened next. I might've lost my temper a little. I might've vented some of my pent-up anger toward the other groups. It was so long ago, I can't be sure, but I might've turned an unhealthy shade of red, shot to my feet, and stormed off screaming, "Fuck those groups!"

I do know that after things had settled down a tad, I agreed to place Debra with an SDF dog. I'd wanted the best people as handlers, and Debra would make a great one. Besides, she promised to keep doing the books for the foundation.

OUR SUCCESS AT finding prime search dog candidates made an old issue resurface: we didn't have the money to support the new dogs. I had our pilot program firefighters pack up Ana, Dusty, and Harley into a kind of traveling road show to run agility demonstrations during breaks at local horse races. During intermission, they would scramble out onto the track and set up obstacles, then go get the dogs and run them through the course, then take it all back down. They joked they were the Beverly Hill-billies, carrying all their possessions on the back of a trailer moving from show to show. It wasn't something we could sustain for long.

The numbers were catching up to the foundation. Our fundraising was not expanding. We were surviving month to month. I was still bearing most of the financial brunt and it was not getting any easier. We needed more time to find more donors and raise money. I was never one to lose sleep over money, but looking back, I never really ac-knowledged to myself how close we were to financial collapse.

Everything came to a head in 1997, as John and I went to sign our tax returns. I knew I had spent a lot of money on building the SDF, but I wasn't exactly sure to what extent. I would supplement payments in small increments—$50 for dog food here, a $75 adoption fee there, $150 for the initial vet exam, $125 for our office rent, and so on—so I didn't end up keeping an exact count. I tried to look at it as an investment. We hadn't started the SDF to make money, and I was certain the foundation would succeed with enough time. To my chagrin, I also knew John wasn't aware of how much of the SDF's finan-cial load we'd been shouldering. I wasn't exactly keeping it a secret from him, but let's just say everyone would probably be happier if he didn't see our "charitable contributions" for the year.

John was thorough with finances upfront, so he usually didn't bother checking the CPA-prepared tax returns before he signed. He hadn't in the past. I crossed my fingers this tax season would be the same.

When our tax returns came in the mail, I signed the cover without opening the document and slid the papers over to John, hoping he would follow suit. He was about to sign, then paused. My heart skipped a beat as he opened the booklet and began looking at the numbers. His eyes searched the page and then stopped on a number. Midway down the second page, the largest number on the page by far, was our charitable contributions to the SDF: $44,000 (about $69,205 in 2019 dollars).

For a moment, John said nothing, only stared at the number. Then he seemed to collect his thoughts. He pointed to the number and turned the document so I could see. "This must be an error," he said.

Here we go. I conjured the most delightful smile I could and directed it toward John. "That's no mistake," I said.

For a moment, silence reigned as John processed what I was telling him. I saw the gears spinning behind his eyes— I could almost hear them grinding away. He probably knew he couldn't shut everything down at this point, but he could've asked me to withdraw from the foundation.

He could've refused to support any more financial contributions. I had a mind on me that refused to quit, but anyone who's been married can attest to the difficulties that arise when his or her better half does not support the other's actions. I ran the SDF, but I never underestimated the support John provided in the background. He could've made things very difficult.

Instead, when he regained his bearings, he spoke without a hint of anger. "Wilma," he said. "There's got to be people out there who care as much as you."

And that was it. He said nothing else on the subject. The man had saint-like emotional intelligence. I mean, how would you react if you'd just found out your spouse had spent almost seventy grand on a charity without your knowledge?

The lesson was not lost on me though. If I wanted the best for my dogs and to push the SDF to be an organization with longevity, I would need to find people willing to give as much as I did. We would need to reach people outside of California. If we could show just how valuable these dogs could be, I knew we would succeed. In the meantime, I focused only on making it through one day at a time.

DURING THE SAME time period covered in those tax returns, the United Nations Security Council passed a resolution that would eventually lead to sanctions against the

African nation of Sudan for harboring terrorists. Most notably, Osama bin Laden. It was the beginning of the end for the terrorist leader's safe haven on the African continent and eventually spurred him to move his operations to Afghanistan via Pakistan in May 1996. The move would come to represent the beginning of independent operations by his terrorist group, al Qaeda. Two years later, bin Laden would issue a personal fatwa—a pronouncement according to his interpretation of Islamic Law—claiming that America had declared war against God. In an interview, bin Laden would state his organization's first priority was to kill Americans and that "If the present injustice continues . . . it would inevitably move the battle to American soil."

Eighteen

THE TIPPING POINT

n September 1998, Abby, Jefferson, Duke, and two other candidates entered Sundowners Kennels to learn the ropes from Pluis. Because certain dogs take longer than others, this was essentially our third round of trainees, and for the most part, Pluis had her system down. She knew what it would take for a dog to successfully complete the training, and she really didn't have any concerns about this new crop. That is not to say there weren't challenges.

Abby, Murphy's firstborn, would get in a mood and let Pluis know exactly what she thought of some of the less glamorous training. Direction control—taking hand-signal commands from handlers from one platform to another—was her least favorite. Pluis would give the command and Abby would give her a *fuck you* glare. Pluis does not repeat commands, so she would try to wait Abby out. Abby would only continue glaring, until Pluis had to physically move her over to the other platform. She had to do this multiple times before Abby begrudgingly obeyed. When it came time for obstacles or searching or anything "fun," on the other hand, Abby was phenomenal. She was like the star player who loved playing in games but never wanted to practice fundamentals. But once she realized it was Pluis's way or the highway, Abby had no issue with training.

Jefferson, Abby's brother, with all her confidence but no moodiness, cruised through training, but did have to be calmed down every once in a while. At one training event, one of the future handlers was passing the time twirling the reward tug around his finger. Jefferson, who'd been lying down and now saw the opportunity to grab his toy, launched a sneak attack on the unsuspecting handler. He leapt up and snatched the toy so fast the handler was not able to release it. The loop broke the handler's finger cleanly. Everyone made sure Jefferson was safely put away before clowning with the toys after that, and many handlers switched to toys without looped ends. Nobody ever questioned if Jefferson had the drive to graduate after that incident.

Duke, the indestructible strongman, had some problems as he learned his new craft. As was apparent with his behavior before heading up to Pluis's kennels, he wasn't the most intellectual dog. When the leash came off, Duke seemed to only hear the perpetual litany of *findthepersonandbark-findthepersonandbark*. He was difficult to control, and the emergency stop command—the dog's "emergency brake" for an immediate halt, for the dog and/ or handler's safety, on a rubble pile—was just not a concept he understood. When going fast is so much fun, why would you want to stop? But as with most things, repetition and consistency finally drove the lesson home. Duke eventually became so skilled at the command that his handler would take him to schools to demonstrate a stop-drop-and-roll to children. Duke was also ready to graduate.

WHEN IT CAME time for handler pairing, Debra Tosch was excited for whomever she got, but not being physically large, she probably wouldn't be the best fit for an oxen like Duke, and she might not be the best to keep Jefferson's ego in check. Pluis knew this, too, and the boys went to other handlers. When Debra was handed the leash for little black Abby, Debra's first thought was, *Thank God she's small!* It's a good thing Debra was a quick learner, because Abby came out right away and let her new handler know everything better be right, and right the first time. With the help of the pilot program firefighters, Debra and the other new handlers followed the training-all-the-time protocol. Even though Debra wasn't a firefighter, she stepped up and put herself through the necessary classes to become FEMA task force ready. She knew Abby would accept nothing less than perfection.

And Abby responded in kind. The pair was soon breezing through searches. Abby's movements, dancing like a ballerina across the rubble, bore a striking similarity to the fluid movements of the SDF's first dog and little Golden legend, Ana. And much like Ana, Abby and Debra achieved their FEMA Basic certification just three months after graduating from Pluis's kennel.

Abby became the model for other handlers who were struggling or were in the queue to learn. But that's not to say she lost any of her dramatics. On one training outing, Abby was loaned to another handler whose dog had been struggling and needed a break. But not long after the swap, the handler approached Debra with some disturbing news: there was something wrong with Abby. He informed her Abby was searching slow and awkwardly. The handler demonstrated, giving Abby the search command. Abby obeyed, but as the handler had described, she was about half her normal speed and lethargic, almost like she was sick. Debra called Abby back and looked her over. She rubbed down Abby's shiny black coat. Nothing seemed amiss. Abby was alert and happy. Then Debra ran through her normal pre-search routine and gave Abby the search command. Abby rocketed off, searching perfectly. Debra shook her head in amusement. The other handler had not done something perfectly, so Abby had decided to mess with him. You really had to earn her respect.

Abby wasn't the only one who toyed with handlers. I took it upon myself to do that as well—for their own good, of course. Abby's brother Jefferson had been assigned an equally confident handler. They were a great match and a talented team. But I noticed in one training session I was grading they were getting too confident, too relaxed, while searching. To a degree this is good, but not to the extent they were demonstrating. Comfort breeds complacency, and that can have dire consequences in a real disaster. I needed to up the handler's stress level a bit.

"Watch this," I said to Debra, and walked over to where Jefferson and his handler were suiting up to start their next search. I pulled the handler aside and gave him a concerned look. "Is Jefferson feeling ok?"

The handler was caught off guard. "Yes," he said, nonplussed. Up to this point, he'd thought they were acing the session.

"Hmm," I said, then walked away, leaving the confused handler furiously rerunning every possible mistake he could've made through his mind.

I didn't do this to be cruel. From that point forward, the handler did everything by the book, not letting Jefferson cut any corners, their level of urgency much higher. They continued to excel. In June of 1999, Jefferson and his handler caught up with some of the earlier graduates and passed their FEMA Advanced certification to join Ana, Dusty, Harley, and the Shermanator as ready to deploy in response to a disaster anywhere in the nation.

144   HERO DOGS

IN LATE 1999, Zack, the puppy prodigy and his autodidact handler, Jeff Place, achieved FEMA Advanced certification, making five teams deployable worldwide in just over two years. Then we hit a tipping point. Manny, the neurotic Boarder Collie, certified. Billy, the lithe Black Lab who'd been among our second-round candidates, certified. Sky, another big Black Lab, and his handler certified. Abby, the runt of the litter and Murphy's only girl, joined the flood of candidates in achieving their Advanced certification, making eleven teams total that could deploy worldwide. As the millennium turned, the SDF had thirty-one dogs either with some level of certification, or currently in training.

Our only sad story was Lola, the buckshot-ridden Lab from Tennessee. Lola had graduated from Sundowners and achieved her FEMA Basic certification. Shortly after though, she was diagnosed with Addison's disease and had to retire from searching. Her handler kept Lola close, adopting her as a "normal" pet and sharing medical expenses with the SDF. Lola was given the best care and a loving home for the rest of her years until she passed in 2002.

Nineteen

IRONDOG

N obody wants a disaster to happen, but a critical part of validating our readiness is an actual deployment. Our eleven FEMA Advanced certified teams were training to stay ready. But by early 2000, that was all they'd done—train, constantly and endlessly.

FEMA requires recertification every three years, so Ana and Dusty, having certified in 1997, actually had to recertify to maintain their deployable status. I knew from my Oklahoma City experience that deployment was at a level you can never fully prepare for. We needed a capstone event to get the handlers as close as possible. So we created the IronDog, a SAR canine training event simulating a multi-day disaster response deployment.

In the spring of 2000, with the cooperation of the decommissioned US Army post Fort Ord, we traveled to Monterey, California, with multiple teams. Our philosophy for the workshop followed the adage *train hard, search easy*. The teams faced steep ladders into dilapidated buildings, narrow corridors and confined spaces, and flooded rooms. They had to compete in no-light and low-light searches. They had to search out deep-buried victims, partially buried victims, and no victims. We threw everything we could think of at them. We seeded search areas with live rats and rabbits, food, human clothing and tissue. The handlers were constantly pressured and allowed to sleep very little. We wanted nothing to be a surprise when the day came for the real thing.

The dogs searched brilliantly. They flew through the event, rarely thrown off their game by the multiple gotchas we embedded into the course. There were always improvements to be made, but everyone left comfortable with the level the dogs were searching at and happy to share lessons with their fellow searchers. We knew it was only a matter of time before lives depended on this training.

Twenty

SEPTEMBER 10, 2001

A s John and I boarded a flight to Maui, Hawaii, for what was supposed to be a relaxing vacation, my mind was anything but calm.

Almost four years had passed since the SDF pilot program had successfully FEMA certified Ana, Dusty, and Harley. Our ranks had since swelled to thirty-three teams. We were training dogs faster than it had ever been done before. The SDF had survived over half a decade.

But there was the rub. *Survived.* As an organization, we were still limping along financially, month to month. Our concern wasn't over whether or not we had a nice office with matching stationery; it was always about the dogs. We refused to compromise on quality. We owed our candidate dogs the best training, care, nutrition, vet treatment, and forever homes. We owed our SAR teams unparalleled training. Both of these factors were constant and ever-improving, and they needed a constant revenue stream to support them. Financially, we'd avoided going off the cliff, but we were still very much on the precipice.

I was starting to worry about myself, too. I'd accumulated a few more loyal volunteers, but still had Debra Tosch on as the only part-time employee. I was doing all the training of handlers myself, and traveling over two thousand miles a month. I'd hand over the reins of the foundation to Debra and trek out to a fire station for the night, sleep there, and train during the day. I had a lot of energy, but it was starting to grind me down. I was sixty-seven years old and felt like *I* was a firefighter. Short-handed, the organization suffered with fundraising while I was away, and we always had to claw our way back from a deficit.

Perhaps the biggest blow of all was when John, the man who'd stood beside me through all my crazy trips and slightly above average charitable contributions, the man who held down the home front while I threw my heart and soul into training the best search dogs and handlers, was diagnosed with cancer.

John was as strong as they came. He'd done the Ironman Triathlon eleven times. He'd been beside me throughout the entire struggle. He was always there with ideas and support, and now his future was a question mark. I was beginning to think the SDF's future was as well.

As the airplane lifted off the LAX tarmac and our vacation was supposed to begin, I struggled to let go. For the time, I couldn't shake the feeling I was at the end of a fraying rope.

ALMOST HALF A world away, before the sun was rising on the East Coast of the United States, nineteen men from al Qaeda awoke at various nondescript hotels near airports in the northeast. The early morning darkness better concealed the small knives hidden in bags and beneath garments as they filtered out into rented cars and drove to the nearby airports. Five hijackers boarded American Airlines Flight 11 and five boarded United Flight 175 with plans to take over both aircrafts and pilot them into New York City airspace.

By 8:14 a.m., both flights were airborne.

PART II

Twenty-one

SEPTEMBER 11, 2001

awoke to the screech of the phone in our condo. It was a little after 3 a.m. in Maui, Hawaii. "Turn on the television!" the SDF volunteer at the other end of the line told me. I fumbled for the remote in the dark and switched on the TV. On the screen I saw the two World Trade Center towers billowing smoke.

False alarm, I thought. I told the volunteer that New York firefighters specialized in high-rise rescue, and that they would know what to do. There wasn't anything the foundation could provide that the fire departments didn't already have. Then I watched Tower 2 buckle and collapse.

I knew everything had changed. Our dogs were about to head into the storm. All my fatigue from the previous day vanished as I struggled to think of what to do next.

"Call five volunteers from the phone tree," I told the volunteer on the phone. "Have them call one or two others and meet in our office in an hour. I'll call you then and we'll talk about what we're going to do."

I CALLED THE office an hour later and spoke with a small audience of volunteers. We had not received official word our dogs were going—we on the civilian side were very much on the periphery of urgent deployments since, after supplying the dogs, the SDF does not play an active role in deployments—but I knew it was a guarantee. FEMA would need multiple task forces for a disaster of this size.

Over the past years, our volunteers had accumulated various contacts at a plethora of media outlets in an effort to get our message outside of California. Up to this point, they had been for naught. I knew that was about to change. SDF-trained teams were about to embark on what might be the largest rescue operation the nation had ever seen.

I told the volunteers to call every media contact we had a number for and give them the SDF contact information with instructions that while they wouldn't care now, once the dogs hit the rubble pile, they would. I had a friend at the local Ventura radio station that proposed using the station to send a message to all of the station's local affiliates offering interviews with me about the SDF. I said to call me any hour of the day. I didn't know if any of the media outlets would take us seriously, but we didn't have time to care.

The SDF teams had been training over five years to be ready to respond to this call. I knew our teams were ready. But America didn't—not yet. These dogs and firefighters were here to support our nation, and it was the SDF's job to get that message of hope out to the rest of the country.

RICK, RANDY, AND Rob, with the dogs resting comfortably in their crates, rumbled along above thirty thousand feet in a C-5 Galaxy. The massive military transport jet could transport five Bradley Fighting Vehicles, but today only carried vehicles and equipment for FEMA USAR California Task Force 7 out of Sacramento. Not far off the wingtips of the Galaxy lingered two F-16 fighter jets. At this point on September 11, these were some of the only airplanes in the sky over the United States. All civilian aircraft had been grounded. Details coming through to the FEMA task forces were still foggy, but officials knew the four downed airliners had been hijackings and were taking no chances.

If the details of the situation were not apparent to the trio of firefighters, the seriousness was. Those fighters lurking outside the cabin like shadowy sharks were an armed escort. The white cylinders protruding like menacing spears from beneath the fighters' wings weren't dummy rounds; they were real air-to-air missiles.

The official FEMA word to deploy had come a few hours after the second World Trade Center tower fell. Rick Lee had been on an all-night call (non-search-related), and had to scramble home to get Ana and join his task force teammates. At Travis Air Force Base they loaded the military jet.

Rick was nervous, but not to the point of worry—the years of disciplined training, the methodical sharpening of the blade, day after day, warranted no need. The job was the only thing he needed to focus on. At six years old, Ana was actually entering the twilight of her searching years, but she hadn't slowed yet. Rick had no apprehension about what they would inevitably be called to do, and knew that they'd need Ana at her very best for it.

An uneasy restlessness hovered around the members of the task force as the C-5 sped on through the night. Everybody wanted to talk about what they were flying into, but nobody really knew what that was, so few words were exchanged.

For the three Goldens, this was just as well—less distraction as the dull roar of jet engines lulled them into sleep. A few years ago nobody believed these dogs would amount to anything; now an entire task force prayed they had.

BLACK LAB ABBY and Debra Tosch were training when the towers collapsed. The problem was that their training class wasn't in the same place as the rest of their FEMA task force when the order came to deploy.

Abby and Debra, along with Abby's rival Lab, Billy; Border Collie Manny; fearless Chocolate Lab Duke; as well as four other canine teams and their respective handlers were all in Seattle attending a FEMA training class. With all commercial flights grounded, they had no way to get home in time. Their home task forces, Sacramento and Los Angeles, were already mobilizing to deploy within a few hours.

Debra and the other handlers pleaded with FEMA officials to get them a flight, but inter-state coordination was not as fluid back then. The best officials could offer would be a reassignment to a second-wave task force, San Diego Task Force 8, deploying in a few days, but the canine teams would need to get back within California state lines. The clock was ticking.

The handlers consulted briefly and decided they would do whatever it took to make the deployment. They crammed eight dogs, eight handlers, and all their equipment into the two largest rental vans they could find, and left the Space Needle and a cloudy Seattle sky in their dust.

Twenty-two

SEPTEMBER 12, 2001

A na, Dusty, and Harley, along with the Three Rs, touched down at McGuire Air Force Base, New Jersey, at midnight. The base was abuzz as they unloaded the task force's gear. Armed guards stalked around everywhere, shining flashlights and checking IDs. The handlers were told not to leave their barracks without a partner. Nobody knew if another attack was coming.

In a small cement barracks, the dogs went back to sleep right away. Rick and Rob were crammed into one room together, with one bed and one cot. Rob won the seniority game and got the bed. It was 3:00 a.m. by the time Rick locked in the final piece of his military cot and settled in for two hours of sleep.

At 5:00 a.m., alarm clocks went off and the task force assembled for breakfast and a briefing for the day. They would head to Ground Zero to set up a base of operations (BOO) as soon as the buses arrived. Nobody could say exactly when that would be, so the firefighters took the dogs out to do some obedience and search work. They wanted it to be like training, one more repetition on just another day, so as to keep the dogs—and probably their own minds—focused.

The dogs were moving well, but during the trial searches on some abandoned housing near the barracks, they would alert bark on what appeared to be nothing. The firefighters were confused until a bleary-eyed soldier appeared and informed them the dogs' alert barks were waking up the individuals inside. Apparently the housing was not abandoned. The firefighters apologized, but were happy the dogs weren't off their game.

AFTER A LONG wait, a convoy of charter buses arrived and the task forces loaded up. With a heavy police and military escort, they drove north on the deserted New Jersey Turnpike through Newark. The dogs slept. The firefighters did not. The bus was quiet as everyone stayed within their own minds. Then New York City came into view. The famous skyline, whose silhouette graced T-shirts and coffee mugs and was imprinted on the minds of people worldwide as a symbol of prosperity in America, stretched across the horizon in front of them. Except in this picture, above the towering skyscrapers rose a large column of black smoke.

"There it is," someone said.

The quiet bus cut to absolute silence. This was why they were here. No one else spoke as the bus continued on to the Javits Convention Center in Manhattan, where the task forces would set up their BOO. The smell of smoke permeated the air. As the firefighters unloaded the dogs and set up their equipment, the mood was somber. Everyone would've much rather gotten straight to work on the rubble pile.

THE CONVENTION CENTER quickly became its own city. Tents were erected everywhere to house the FEMA task forces. Thirteen task forces from throughout the country joined the six from California. Search dogs are only a small part of the team. A FEMA task force consists of about seventy cross-trained individuals who serve in rescue, medical, hazardous materials, logistics, and planning, and includes technical specialists such as physicians and structural engineers in addition to the canine teams. These specialists bring in a wide array of tools—listening devices, fiber-optic cameras, and extraction equipment—that all complement the dog searches.

The specialized units were housed in the same area, so all the canine teams were put together. The tents were packed so tightly they practically overlapped. It was four to a tent, two slept while two searched. The lights were always on, and only a thin curtain separated the teams from the constant roar of machinery bringing in personnel and supplies.

The task forces were organized into shifts. Randy and Dusty and Rick and Ana were paired together on the graveyard shift; Rob and Harley were on dayshift with a civilian from another task force. Because it was already late in the day, the graveyard shift would be up first. Rick and Randy began to prep their Goldens, who, at this point, were raring to get the search started.

AT 5:00 P.M. eastern time, Ana and Dusty and their handlers boarded a charter bus for their first search of Ground Zero. As the bus left the convention center, a mass of New Yorkers staged outside the fences surged forward, cheering and shouting and waving flags and signs, anything they could do to boost the rescuers' morale. Rick felt like they were cheering their favorite movie star. The mass of people would remain there, twenty-four hours a day, for every day of the rescue mission. In return, the firefighters wrote their task force name and home state on the side of the bus to show the locals that the whole nation was here to help.

The bus left the cheering crowd and maneuvered through the streets toward Ground Zero with a heavy military escort. They moved through ever-tightening cordons of US Army, US Marshals, NYPD, and NY State Troopers. As they approached Ground Zero, the colors seemed to fade away into monochrome, almost like they were traveling back in time. Gray dust covered streets and walls, signs and windows. Abandoned cars were everywhere. It was like New York City had vanished and they were now traveling through a ghost town.

Eventually, the bus made it as far as it could go. The rest would be on foot. Rick led Ana down the aisle and stepped off onto what appeared to be the surface of the moon. Thick dust, almost a half-foot deep, sucked up his boots as he stepped from the door. Everything was dirty almost immediately. Ana and Dusty stood fast as their handlers donned protective gear. The firefighters put on kneepads and helmets with headlamps and chemical glow lights on the back for identification in the dark. They duct-taped the top of their boots so the dust wouldn't pour in their feet. They donned masks to filter the floating ash and wore gloves. Randy put an American flag bandana around his neck. With utility belts over their blue FEMA Task Force jumpsuits, they clipped on flashlights and radios to communicate with one another, and waist packs with medical supplies and water for the dogs. They kept notepads and search checklists and pens in their breast pockets. In their side pockets were the fire hose toys for the dogs, ready to reward. The dogs wore nothing; they carried everything they needed in their noses, minds, and hearts. Then the teams trudged through the moon dust toward an intersection that spilled light like a beacon in the dark.

As they rounded the corner, they saw it. Absolute destruction stretching out in small mountain ranges, maze on top of maze of twisted steel. Some I beams and H beams interconnected, others jutting out at odd angles like a poorly woven rug. Smoke billowed in huge white plumes from its center—there were places where the rubble was still smoldering. A large area was bathed in the pale sheen of floodlights, casting monstrous shadows and giving the mangled metal an otherworldly look. Outside the lights, solitary shafts of steel stuck up from the rubble at unnatural angles, like masts of sunken ships.

It wasn't just the two trademark towers that fell. The World Trade Center (WTC) was actually composed of seven separate buildings, including a Marriott hotel and an underground mall connecting the sixteen acres. On the side of the rubble nearest to the dogs and firefighters, an exterior frame of what had been WTC Building 7, once forty-seven stories high, leaned defiantly at a thirty-degree angle like a wayward fence post. Everything on the frame was stripped away except the steel skeleton, the empty window frames staring back at the rescue workers like rows of unblinking eyes.

A charter bus that had been parked on the street was crushed flat like it'd been made of cardboard. Other vehicles shared the same fate. Among the dust were smatterings of papers with letterheads—stationery from corporate offices that had once rested somewhere in the WTC Tower's 110 stories. Other than the paper, there was only steel and dust. There was not a single piece of office furniture. No computers or printers. No carpets. No glass. Besides the scattered pieces of main support shafts from lower stories, there was no concrete. Everything but the steel seemed to have been thrown into a 1,350-foot blender and crushed into the fine powder now at the firefighters' feet.

Heavy machinery was everywhere, hauling debris. All structures on the WTC land collapsed or were irreparably damaged. Surrounding buildings, streets, and vehicles were also damaged by each collapse, which registered as about a 2.0 magnitude earthquake on the Richter scale. All in all, close to two million tons of building either hit the ground that day or were pulverized to dust.

On the rubble pile, things were moving slow. Firefighters and police and some civilians were stretched in long lines across the debris field. They would fill five-gallon buckets with as much rubble as possible, and then hand it down the line in an old-fashioned bucket brigade. They were desperate, their breath pouring long jets of steam into the frigid air, no doubt making little progress and feeling powerless to do anything about it. Rick and Randy knew the dogs could help give direction to this search, and focus rescue efforts. If the area was clear, these rescuers could move on to a place that might not be.

Rick and Randy requested permission, and a short time later, a call came over the radio that the canine teams were cleared to search.

Rick and Randy maneuvered Ana and Dusty down the pile toward the leaning wall of Building 7 in order to allow the dogs to get deep into the debris pile. The pile was so big, covering multiple city blocks and many stories deep, that they would only search small portions at a time. They watered the dogs and wiped them down the best they could. Then it was time to search. Dusty was up first. Randy glanced across the devastating scene one more time then released his partner.

The dog who just a few years ago was headed for a shelter, the submissive Golden Retriever who shied away from a raised voice and clutched anyone nice enough to give her affection, now leapt forward without hesitation, leading the rescue effort for the largest terrorist attack in history.

The search got off to a bumpy start. Even though the dogs had been exercised, the nervous energy that had surrounded everything for days gave them an extra boost. As Dusty shot out of the gate, she jumped onto an I beam with a little too much zest. The beam was thick with powdered debris and immediately Dusty started to slide. Randy watched, horrified, as his partner started to skid toward the edge of the beam that stretched multiple stories above the ground. But all those days training on the wobbly monster with Pluis paid off. Dusty did not panic;

she shifted her weight and spread her paws. Her skid slowed, then stopped. Randy was able to breathe again. After that, Dusty didn't miss a beat. She bounded through the treacherous terrain like she was walking on air. Randy tried to keep his eye on her, but most of his commands had to be given remotely since the footing was so impassable for humans. No problem for Dusty, who was used to receiving only hand signals. She made her way over the exterior of the collapsed building then disappeared down a hole leading deep inside the sharp mess of steel.

Randy stayed focused on the spot, but behind him Rick noticed a change in the atmosphere around them. Looking around, he saw why. The entire search area had gone quiet as every rescue worker on the pile was now watching the search. It was as if someone had muted the whole scene as the rescue workers held their breath and prayed, silently willing Dusty to strike gold and uncover a live victim.

One minute turned into several. No Dusty. Randy was considering moving to check her, when out of another hole near the top of the pile came a rocket of Golden fur. Dusty perched on top of some steel, tail wagging furiously, staring back at Randy as if to say, *Ok, Dad. What's next?*

Ana searched next, covering the same area as Dusty to be sure it was clear. She leapt from beam to beam, threading her way through the wreckage. She made short work of the area, the same way Dusty had, but also did not alert. Rick broke the news to the onlookers that the dogs had shown no indication of anyone alive in this specific area. Although no victims had been found, no one who saw the dogs search doubted their thoroughness. There would be many more searches and it was much too early to give up hope.

The firefighters took Ana and Dusty back to the search staging area to let them rest and wait for the next assignment. While the dogs relaxed, Rick and Randy returned to the search site near Building 7. The area that just an hour ago was teeming with rescue workers and heavy equipment, saturated with floodlights and noise, was now dark and silent. The entire rescue effort had moved on because of the results from the canine searches. No one was alive here, so the teams focused elsewhere where someone might be. Randy felt a wave of emotion bury him. It was then he really felt the importance of the job he and his dog were doing.

The moment weighed heavy on both firefighters' minds, not with pressure, but reassurance. This was why they had trained so hard, like they were searching for their own families. They knew Ana and Dusty were some of the best search dogs in the nation—*knew* it. They were given this enormous responsibility because they could handle it. Rick remembers it as a galvanizing moment. They were ready for the next mission. Ana and Dusty, of course, were always ready.

Twenty-three

"THEY'RE ALL DEAD."

As Ana and Dusty and Harley worked their way across the Ground Zero rubble piles, I was still in Hawaii, but hadn't left the condo since the towers collapsed. Meanwhile, the phones at our tiny Ojai office were ringing off the hook. People were clamoring for updates about the dogs and more information about the foundation. People also began asking the question I had been asking long ago—why did America have so few search dogs? People began to give selflessly. Some donations were small, some large, but everybody gave. It was too late to affect the current deployment, but they knew that when the next disaster hit, we couldn't be left asking that same question.

The SDF was used to a few mailed-in donations a

month. It didn't take more than a day or two for our understaffed and overstretched office to become swamped. We didn't have a robust computer system at the time, so everything was done by hand and voice. What we needed above all else was more phone lines. I tasked a volunteer to get more installed and quickly received a message the phone company couldn't install them until next week.

"Give me the phone guy's number," I said. Our country had just been attacked and fellow Americans were trusting the SDF to take their support seriously. I was in no mood for waiting patiently. When I got the phone guy on the line I bombarded him. "Do you see those dogs on television searching Ground Zero? Those dogs are from our foundation in *our* hometown! They need our support, and we need more phone lines right now. I would say today, but I don't want to sound unreasonable."

The phones were in the next day.

OUT EAST, THE large tank of a dog, Sherman "The Shermanator," arrived at Ground Zero with California Task Force 1, not far behind the Three Rs and the Sacramento Task Force. Because the rest of his teammates had been stranded in Seattle, Sherman and his handler, Steve, were on their own at first. But to a dog that willingly smashes plate glass windows, fear has little meaning. Sherman plowed over the stacks of steel with no apprehension whatsoever. The massive Lab put every ounce of his energy into searching. Steve was always worried Sherman would unintentionally hurt himself. On one search, Sherman was marauding across the steel in his usual take-no-prisoners manner, not slowing or pausing or exhibiting any type of caution. Rain from the night before had made things slick, and the steel was dangerous. Steve wanted to get control of Sherman before the dog crashed. As Steve moved to get closer, he slipped and fell, smacking his leg. Steve stood up and dusted himself off, contemplating the irony. Sherman, on the other hand, didn't even blink and went right on searching. He knew his job and he let nothing distract him.

Despite his all-business attitude on the pile, Sherman was quick to make friends. Firefighters and other rescue workers on the day shift were always petting him and using his big frame as a buoy while they crossed the debris. Sherman, ever a gentle giant, never grew tired of it. He seemed to understand everybody needed support right now.

IN THE FOLLOWING days, as they waited for search assignments, Ana and Dusty would rest as Rick and Randy accompanied the reconnaissance team across Ground Zero. Sometimes they'd be joined by FDNY Firefighters. They would walk for hours through the destruction. Block after block, windows were blown out and walls were pocked with holes and charred scars. Any trees left standing had been stripped of leaves; now only tiny scraps of shredded paper hung in their branches like morbid ornaments. Thick dust coated everything. The firefighters felt like an infantry platoon patrolling across a war-torn Europe in World War II. They would pass other firefighters, just standing disconsolately, shell-shocked, as they tried to piece together what had happened. Others were near collapse with exhaustion and grief, having lost countless brothers in an instant, yet refusing to rest.

Rick remembers going through an alleyway not far from their BOO whose wall was completely covered in missing-persons photographs. An entire wall of silent faces looking out at the rescuers, notes from loved ones scrawled along the edges, pleading for information about the missing individual.

The search teams found FDNY fire engines, abandoned and silent. Some had been crushed beyond recognition. Others were unharmed, save for a thick layer of dust. Rick and Randy passed one such engine still in its staging position and undamaged, having been shielded from the collapse by one of the nearby high-rises. There were messages scrawled in the layer of dust on the windows from other firefighters. "God Bless," one message read. As they passed the engine, their FDNY escort broke from the recon team and trudged over to the engine. He opened the engine's door and looked inside at the crew tag, which listed the engine's crew members. He stood still for a minute, holding the door and reading the names.

Then he shut it. Dust billowed off in a small cloud. He returned to the team, his face stiff with a tortured agony. "They're all dead," he said. The group continued in silence. Behind them, the trucks hauling debris rumbled on.

Twenty-four

THE STORM AND THE QUESTION

Ana and Dusty were back in action on the next graveyard shift. Rick and Randy led the two dogs around the debris of Building 4, what used to be the Commodities Exchange building standing nine stories high. Rick paused with Ana and noticed the large antenna that used to top Building 4, now sticking up through the debris like a compound fracture. Someone had hung an American flag atop it. The red, white, and blue blazed against the monochrome background and pale floodlights. The wind whipped our nation's colors back and forth in the cold night sky. It was then Rick realized he hadn't checked the weather report for the evening. Because of the floodlights, they couldn't see the sky, but there was certainly a storm coming.

They entered the command post on Church Street, where there was an excited buzz in the air. The recon team was forming up along with a full rescue squad. Two FDNY breathing apparatuses and a helmet had been found in the debris and they needed a specific area searched by the dogs. By the time the second plane hit the tower, twenty-three FDNY Engine companies and thirteen FDNY Ladder companies were responding to the disaster. Before the towers collapsed, over one-third of the entire eleven-thousand-member FDNY was deployed to the WTC. Of the 2,973 Americans killed that day, 343 were firefighters.

Everyone moved with a distinct purpose. Nobody wanted to say the firefighters were alive. Everything up to now indicated that anything that wasn't made of steel had turned into dust. The chances were slim, but even the slightest glimmer of hope that they could recover some of their brothers' remains was incentive enough. The FDNY battalion chief, his voice tight with anticipation, gave the order to move to the search area.

The two teams, flanked by Ana and Dusty, moved along Church Street. They were quick, but in everyone's mind it felt like slow motion. On a different day, in a different place, the squad knew it could've been any one of them buried in the rubble.

The teams worked around a blackened Building 5, burned out by the raging fire after the towers collapsed. They turned the corner down Vesey Street, west toward the Hudson River and what remained of Building 6. They passed a bookstore, its books now layered with dust and shattered glass. Through the patchwork of floodlights loomed another mountain of debris, almost five stories high, shattered steel sticking out in all directions like a collection of giant kitchen knives. Near the end of Building 5 were two intact-but-stagnant escalators leading up to the second story of the debris. At the top, the teams entered a day care. Like the bookstore, the school was intact, but its pastel colors and children's toys now wore the tired and familiar hue of dust and charcoal. Its floors were paved with shattered glass. Every floor above it was a charred mess that had been consumed by fire.

Finally, the teams came to a stop. Dusty and Ana were put into a down-stay. They reluctantly complied, eager to get to searching. The firefighters didn't share the same enthusiasm. In front of them, the path to the specific search area was a chaotic collection of steel, sheared into spikes of all angles and sizes. The only way through was a specific path over unstable footholds, deep voids, and foot traps that threatened to grab anyone walking across. The path, which creaked and groaned underfoot, bordered a two-story crater with a floor of sharp steel.

The teams staged near a blown-out window. Dusty and

Randy would be up first. To begin the search, Dusty would have to be lifted out of the window and up about five feet to the rubble pile that bordered the drop-off.

With one firefighter lifting from the bottom, one pulling from the top, and the other team members doing their best to prevent Randy and Dusty from making the terminal velocity fall down into the crater below, the operation began. There was no room for error. There was also no time to waste. If the buried firefighters had somehow survived the collapse, every second would count toward pulling them out. An inch at a time, Dusty, tail wagging and ready, was hoisted up into position. Ana and Rick and the rest of the team waited on stable ground. They would be unable to see the search.

The FDNY battalion chief led the way, showing Randy where to step. The intermittent flashes from headlamps and flashlights created even more layers on the unstable surface. Each step sent pieces of debris shifting, some spinning off into the black void of the crater. Dust and ash floated in the air in a gray fog. The acrid smell of burned material hung around everything.

The actual search area was small. A twenty-by-twenty square of what remained of the floor of an office building. They were to search the corner, where one exterior wall still stood facing the crater and another wall stood facing the street. To the team's front was all the destruction and debris, and the huge crater. They were literally searching on the edge of a cliff. The two firefighters' breathing apparatuses had been found leaning against the interior wall. The bright yellow oxygen tanks and connecting hoses were equipment Randy was all too familiar with. It was a stark reminder of what was at stake for this search, and it overshadowed any danger.

Randy held Dusty and checked her long line they'd attached for safety. On the other side of the massive crater, he saw more offices, half destroyed. He noticed a steady wind to his front, coming over the crater—it would play tricks with any scents in the area. More troubling, he noticed high atop the building's remaining walls, almost right above them, hung sharp slabs of metal. When the towers had come down, they'd littered the surrounding rooftops with a collection of loose steel. These giant ax blades now hung unsecured and ready to fall. Widowmakers.

The chief and other team members stood back. It was Dusty's show now. Considering the terrain and wind and drop-off into the crater, Randy prepared to release his girl for the most difficult and most dangerous search she'd ever done.

With their focus on the immediate surroundings, the team couldn't see that above them, the night sky was darkening further into a menacing storm.

THE CALL OF "Dog on the pile" came across the radio as Dusty began to search the precarious rubble. She moved her paws quickly, instinctively testing the twisted metal for hot spots or subtle shifts in stability. The steady wind blew around her, spinning dust and ash and mixing scents. She picked her way across the steel sheared into sharp blades and rebar warped into crescents, wary of the multi-story drop that bordered the search area.

Randy watched as Dusty suddenly hooked her head toward the precipice. She paused and sampled the air. A slight tail wag but no alert bark. She had caught the scent of something over the edge, but not enough to alert. Still, the interest was of note. Dusty didn't show that kind of behavior unless there was some legitimacy to the scent. It was worth bringing in a second nose.

Dusty was pulled back and Randy went to consult Rick, who was still waiting with Ana on the ledge a few feet below. Rick prepped Ana to search.

Rick and Ana picked their way across the ledge and over to the window. "Wait," Rick commanded Ana, then, "Lift," as he hoisted her up the few feet to the search area. As he did, he felt the debris beneath his right foot give way. He started to fall. The firm hand of the rescue squad leader, who'd been spotting the movement for exactly this reason, clamped onto Rick's jacket and steadied him. Rick looked down to see shards of metal spill off the edge of the drop and float momentarily before crashing into the ground below. He tried to push that image out of his mind and finished lifting Ana up onto the search plane. The search manager, who'd been waiting up top, grabbed Ana and secured her, then helped Rick up.

Rick studied the scene. He saw the forty-foot-diameter crater where Dusty had shown interest. He thought back to the lessons of the smoke machine and the thousands of hours of training. With the wind and offices on the other side of the hole, there were many places where scent could originate or be spirited in from. Pinpointing a source in this environment would be difficult. Rick checked Ana's safety line, then released her. "Search!"

Ana quickly made her way around the corner toward the edge. Rick followed slowly. He had to hug the wall to keep from slipping over the edge. Ana worked closer and closer to the edge of the crater. Then she stopped. She stood, facing the crater, and started barking so hard her entire body shook.

Rick knew this type of bark meant Ana had something, but needed to get closer to the scent to be sure. He wouldn't call an alert yet, but it didn't stop his heart from hammering away in his chest. The problem in this case was getting closer meant going over the edge of a cliff. Somewhere in the depths of the crater, there could be victims, but there were other factors to consider as well. On the other side of the massive hole were more offices, some still intact. The wind was playing odd tricks in the area and could be carrying scents across the void and into Ana's nose. There could be buried victims, or it might just be another search party that they couldn't see. Before committing a rescue team and bringing in heavy resources—an undertaking that would take hours—they would need to clear the office building across the crater and eliminate it as a source. Ana and Dusty could certainly make that determination, but until they gave their true bark alert, the team had more investigating to do. A search specialist and hazmat expert split from the team and made their way to the offices on the other side of the crater in an attempt to eliminate some of the possibilities of the scent.

Rick conferred with Randy. Given the unlikeliness of someone surviving the collapse and the fact that no one had been found alive up to this point, their gut feeling was that the wind was probably carrying in the scent from a live rescuer from elsewhere. They decided to search the office once they got the OK from the search specialist, and then focus on the bottom of the crater itself.

The dog teams made their way back out through the day care and down the escalators and out onto the main rubble pile. As carefully and quickly as possible, they began picking their way across the felled steel. They listened for calls on the radio from their recon element and tried to stay positive. No calls came. Ana and Dusty did not show any interest in the lower areas near the crater, either.

Besides the scrapes of claws and boots across steel, a few muffled coughs and heavy breaths, there was no sound. The whole of New York City, it seemed, had gone silent.

Then they heard it. It was a barely perceptible rise in pressure that grew quickly into the whistle of wind. The whistle grew into a roar as a strong microburst whipped through the windowless holes and collapsed walls of Buildings 5 and 6. The angled steel widowmakers that hung like deadly icicles off the roofs of the building began to rattle. As the wind grew, the steel began to rumble in a sinister percussion section of war drums. Then the sky split with a matching thunder of its own. The storm was here.

The search party was momentarily frozen as again and again the sky boomed with thunder. Within seconds, small pieces of metal began to fall from the surrounding rooftops. The heavens opened up and a torrent of rain poured down onto the stranded searchers, turning the ash and dust into a thick mud. Lightning temporarily bleached the sky white. The giant steel widowmakers began to swing and sway, then fall to earth.

Across the radios came the frantic command for the immediate evacuation of the search area. Everyone knew what this would mean for another search for life in the crater. Randy remembers Rick, a soaked and muddy Ana huddled against his side, screaming over the rain and thunder that they needed to get down in the crater and search it.

The call for evacuation came again. They couldn't risk the lives of the dogs or more firefighters on a mere possibility. There was only one option. Rick and Randy made what they would recall as one of the most difficult decisions they've ever faced, and abandoned the search.

They grabbed their dogs and the team retreated back into the building, leaving behind only questions as huge blades of steel crashed into the ground around them like giant guillotines.

THE DOGS AND the firefighters sat in the dark among the sludge and broken glass on the floor of the abandoned day care, waiting for the storm to pass. Their boots were caked with cement-gray sludge. Some NYPD officers had passed up poster boards from the bookstore through a broken window so the dogs wouldn't have to lie in the mud. Ana and Dusty snuggled up against their handlers for warmth. Rick wrapped Ana in a small blanket from the Salvation Army. Normally, she would rip up blankets, but for one reason or another she adopted this one—she would use it for the rest of her life. Outside the rain poured and the thunder boomed. A few floodlights cast ghostly illumination on the soaked and shattered landscape outside. Nobody spoke.

Eventually word came down. The weather wasn't letting up and there was no break forecasted. For now, all searches were cancelled. The site was too dangerous. The incoming shift would search that same area of interest as soon as it was safe.

Ana and Rick Lee rappel into a search dog demonstration in California.
Rick Lee

A young Wilma with her dog, Toffee.
Wilma Melville

Wilma with her young star, Murphy.
Wilma Melville

Wilma poses with Ana, the first candidate for the Search Dog Foundation.
Rick Lee

Harley, Dusty, and Ana, the three original SDF dogs, prepare for training at Sundowners Kennel in Gilroy, California. *Randy Gross*

Ana in her princess pool, celebrating FEMA Canine Search certification.
Rick Lee

Dogs and handlers pose for a hero shot after a training session. The Hummer in the background is not standard issue (unfortunately). *Rick Lee*

Wilma shows Dusty some love after a training search. *Randy Gross*

The stars of the show pose for a group photo at our IronDog training event. *Rick Lee*

Dusty practices rappelling into isolated search areas during training. *Randy Gross*

Dusty climbs the ladder with Randy right behind her. *Randy Gross*

Dusty wears her fire department badge with pride. *Randy Gross*

Ana, Dusty, and Harley rest before a search in New York City after 9/11. *Randy Gross*

Dusty and Randy head into Ground Zero. Notice the difficulty of the terrain they are negotiating. *Randy Gross*

Dusty and Randy making their way through the endless steel maze in Ground Zero. *Randy Gross*

Ana and the search teams cross the ghostly remains of the WTC plaza. The scarred golden globe at the edge of the photo is the "Sphere for Plaza Fountain," the only piece of art to survive the 9/11 attacks. *Rick Lee*

Ana and the team during a crater search on Ground Zero. This photo gives a good idea of the magnitude of the search area. *Rick Lee*

Ana takes a breather between searches at Ground Zero. *Rick Lee*

Randy takes time to thank his loyal partner after a search on Ground Zero. *Randy Gross*

Randy's new "Black Lab." Dusty on her way to a decon bath after swimming through oil during a subway search. *Randy Gross*

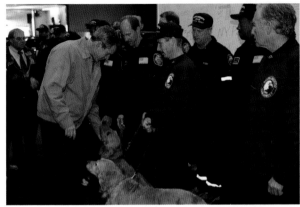

Ana and Dusty meet President George W. Bush. *Randy Gross*

Dusty closes the New York Stock Exchange: The first "real" dog to perform the task. *Randy Gross*

Ana tries to stay cool between searches in Mississippi after
Hurricane Katrina. Notice the massive amount of wood in
the rubble. *Rick Lee*

Dusty searches through an ocean of splinters in the
aftermath of Hurricane Katrina. *Randy Gross*

Dusty and Randy prepare for some training with an aerial insertion via helicopter. *Randy Gross*

Ana training on a fire department ladder. Even in her later years, Ana's agility was exceptional. *Rick Lee*

Abby and her longtime handler, Debra Tosch. *Karen L. Newbill*

Cody was returned by seven homes before being rescued by the SDF. Now look at that tail-high confidence. *Karen L. Newbill*

Cody crosses the high balance beam with ease at SDF demonstration. *Karen L. Newbill*

High energy is a must for any search dog. *Karen L. Newbill*

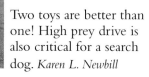

Two toys are better than one! High prey drive is also critical for a search dog. *Karen L. Newbill*

Physical ability is the third key ingredient for a search dog. Here a search dog (with no shortage of physical ability) takes a shortcut over the wobbly monster obstacle. *Karen L. Newbill*

An SDF volunteer tests a shelter dog for prey drive to see if he could potentially be a search dog . . . *Karen L. Newbill*

. . . And after successfully passing the screening tests, a search dog candidate starts his journey from rescued to rescuer! *Karen L. Newbill*

A search dog trains on a low balance beam. The dogs start low and go higher as their confidence grows. *Karen L. Newbill*

Search dogs often need to wait for a command from their handler before executing obstacles. Here a search dog waits—rather picturesquely— for the command to descend a ladder. *Karen L. Newbill*

Another handsome search dog waits for the command to dismount a stack of crates. *Karen L. Newbill*

Posing for the media is part of the job. Here a shy search dog poses on the back of a fire engine. *Karen L. Newbill*

A whole crew of search dogs posing on the fire engine. *Karen L. Newbill*

Wilma gets some love from her fans. *Karen L. Newbill*

Ana enjoys her retirement and helping Rick Lee put up Christmas lights during the holidays. *Rick Lee*

Hollywood Hunter. *Karen L. Newbill*

Billy gives one of many interviews with Hunter. Hunter has his own fan in the background. *Karen L. Newbill*

They can walk the walk, too. Hunter and Billy climb a ladder during a training search. *Karen L. Newbill*

The leading ladies of the SDF—Debra, Wilma, and Pluis—wearing red, and backed by the dogs and handlers in blue. *Karen L. Newbill*

Where it all began: Rob Cima, Rick Lee, and Randy Gross pose with Wilma and the dogs at an SDF ceremony. The only one missing is Harley, who had recently passed away. In his stead was Ace, a tough Lab who'd survived abuse and abandonment, and now served proudly with Rob. *Randy Gross*

As the teams rose to begin their trek back to the BOO, they tried to make sense of what had just happened. Had there been victims buried in that crater or somewhere in the surrounding offices? If so, why had the fates intervened to pull them off of the search? They were questions that would probably never be answered.

A FEW HOURS later, Harley and Rob Cima, on dayshift, made ready to check the area where Ana and Dusty had indicated interest the previous night. The rain had cleared somewhat, but the situation had not improved much. Now, word from the structural engineers was that Building 6 in its entirety was going to collapse—they just couldn't say when. All they could predict was that when it did, it would fall in the direction of Vesey Street. Rob didn't find much comfort in that information and made a mental note to stay off Vesey Street.

Harley had to be fully harnessed and roped up for the search. The crater was lined with deep, multistory crevasses lined with razor-sharp pieces of steel, and surrounded by a building ready to collapse. Because of the danger, only one additional firefighter accompanied the search team.

When they were in a somewhat stable position, Rob surveyed the search area. There wasn't much to the small area. But the numerous voids, the holes in the standing walls, and the dust and smoke all made for strange scent patterns. After Ana and Dusty's searches, Rick and Randy had briefed Rob on the direction the dogs had indicated. They were fairly certain the other factors were bringing the live scent of rescue workers at other locations into that area, but they couldn't be sure. This was now days after the towers came down, so the already minimal chances of someone surviving beneath the rubble were cut even further. With so many factors in play, the search teams needed to eliminate all other possibilities before they called in a recovery team and put more lives at risk.

Rob released Harley to search, but purposely sent him in the direction opposite of where the other dogs had shown interest. Rob wanted a completely unbiased search. Harley worked his way across the mangled steel in his methodical-but-unstoppable way. Almost immediately he turned back and headed toward the area Ana and Dusty had indicated live scent. Then he started barking.

Rob called Harley back. The other firefighter looked at Rob, his eyes wide with hope. Rob told him to hold off on the radio call. He sent Harley out again. He had to be sure. Harley went to the same spot again and started his alert bark.

Rob now faced a decision. Because of the ledges and voids, there were still too many places a victim could be buried. Was the victim three stories down at ground level? Below ground? Or nearer the debris surface beneath Harley's paws? How close were the other rescuers that he could not see? Were their scents contaminating the search?

Rob trusted Harley, but the terrain here made for too many questions. They needed to narrow down the area if they were going to have an effective rescue.

Before Rob could contemplate the next step, his radio blared to life—full and immediate evacuation. A sensor had been triggered and the building around them was about to come down.

Rob told the other firefighter to leave. He would need to take his time with Harley. Getting in had been a long, slow struggle, balancing on beams and lifting Harley up high ledges; it had been a fight the entire way. Rob had to carry all the water and equipment usually spread across multiple people. They would not be evacuating quickly. The firefighter obeyed and made his way out of the rubble. Then it was just Rob and Harley and the building that was about to collapse.

Carefully, the team made their way over the debris. Rob kept an eye on the building. There was no way to tell how long the structure would stay standing. He stayed focused on getting out safely so Harley would do the same. One step after the other.

They wove through the partial walls that turned them around like a maze, and finally dumped them out onto a street. Buzzing with activity earlier, the place was now deserted. Harley and Rob walked alone. Then Rob realized why. They were on Vesey Street, the predicted trajectory of the building collapse.

Rob stayed calm. If the building was coming down, it

was coming down. He didn't need Harley picking up on the stress.

A couple hundred yards in the distance, Rob made out the cross street, outside of the collapse zone. That was safety. Rob and Harley trudged toward it. Through the shrouding morning fog and dust, he could see a street lined with hundreds of firefighters and rescue workers. Rob and Harley were the last ones out. When the other firefighters saw Rob, they started screaming at him to hurry.

Despite the screams, Rob continued pressing forward at an even, consistent pace. With all the equipment weighing him down, it was like walking in cement boots. He couldn't run, only lumber forward. The firefighters continued to scream. It was like the final stretch of a marathon and Harley and Rob were the only competitors.

Rob continued his steady Frankenstein walk and Harley high-stepped through the mud on the street. One paw after the other. The building stayed up. Closer and closer. Finally, Rob and Harley were pulled off the street and into safety by the welcoming arms of their brothers.

THE "ALL CLEAR" came a few hours later. As it turned out, the seismic sensor had been set too close to the building and given a false alert. Everyone was frustrated by the mistake as it had cost the recovery effort hours of valuable time.

Harley, still ready to search after the hellish sprint for

life earlier that morning, followed Rob back to the same area. They needed to determine once and for all what was triggering the alert in the debris. This time, the team went underground. They tunneled their way through a dark labyrinth of subterranean floors until they were below the spot Harley had alerted. They were now deep in the rubble. If there were any chance of narrowing the search area, it would be here.

Rob released Harley to search. Harley started toward the same general direction where he had indicated scent from floors above. The far side of the void was small, but Harley's training made such terrain a cakewalk. But for some reason, Harley stopped and would not continue forward to search the void. Rob had never seen him do this before. He told Harley again to search the area. Harley did not budge. The dog looked like he wanted to obey, but something was holding him back. Rob knew they needed the area searched and grew impatient. Harley had never disobeyed him before, why was he doing so now when they needed him the most? Again, Rob ordered Harley to continue searching. Tentatively, Harley turned and entered the void.

As soon as he entered, he was back out. Something was wrong. Rob called Harley back, now concerned. A closer inspection revealed the issue. The entire area where Harley was supposed to search, the epicenter of where they believed the scent was originating from, was still smoldering. Even days after the collapse, deep underground, the debris continued to burn. Harley had sensed the heat and refused to proceed. When he tried, the hot steel started burning his paws.

Rob felt terrible for pushing Harley into the void, but the tough dog had only mildly singed his paws and was still ready to search. Rob was not taking any chances. The area was too dangerous. He scooped up Harley and carried him all the way out to be checked by the vet.

Harley was exhausted from the ordeal, but not seriously injured. Exhausted as well, Rob sat on the muddy curb with Harley under a cold and foggy sky. He covered his partner with a blanket. His shaggy "alley dog" was caked with mud and soot, his Golden fur clumped into thick ropes of black, brown, and gray that stuck out in different directions. The dog moved only his eyes, resting his tired and sore body. He had given everything on the job today, literally searching through a smoldering hellhole, and still his eyes looked to Rob, ready to search again if his handler willed it.

In that moment, there wasn't anything more on earth Rob could've asked of his loyal partner.

IT WOULD BE a long time before the crater cooled enough for anyone to search. As far as the Three Rs knew, there was never another indication of live scent in the area. There would eventually be human remains found near the area of interest, but no one found alive or with any indication that they had been alive beyond the collapse. Maybe the wind tunneled the scent of other rescuers up through the area, or the heat from below the crater dispersed a life-like scent upward that the dogs picked up on. The possibilities are infinite.

Perhaps even more mysterious is the strange string of coincidences that prevented the teams from searching beyond the dog's initial indications. Nobody can explain why the universe seemed pitted against a thorough search of the area.

None of the rescuers dwelled on the event. There was too much more work to do.

Twenty-five

DOWN WE GO

n the next few days, the search expanded beyond the surface rubble and down underground. The dogs would be going into the mall, the subways, and any tunnels large enough to fit them. The WTC mall was composed of eighty stores and connected with terminals for the subway and Port Authority trains that crossed the Hudson. There were plenty of places someone could have survived, but any that did had already left under their own power. No trapped victims had been found alive yet.

Dayshift would lead the first sweep of the mall. It would be different from a normal rubble search as they would be sweeping through only partially collapsed rooms, looking for people trapped in individual areas instead of across a large pile.

Harley and Rob Cima and a small recon team passed flyers informing searchers to be on the lookout for the airlines' black boxes as they descended away from the daylight. They arrived on the mall level. The sprawling shopping grounds that used to see thousands of shoppers daily were silent and the air stale. The only light came from flashlights and a few forks of sunlight reflected down elevator shafts that, just a few days earlier had spewed a conflagration of burning jet fuel. The polished tile floors were now covered with thick dust and scattered debris.

Harley, in his determined and tireless way, walked point. He led the team quietly past a statue of Bugs Bunny, now powder coated and ghostlike in front of a tattered Warner Bros. gift shop. A clock in a jewelry store stood behind shattered windows, frozen at 9:10.

Harley searched the abandoned stores and other rooms, the team behind him making a diagonal line with bright orange paint on the storefront as they entered, and completing an X with another diagonal line as they exited. In areas they couldn't access, the team would snake in fiber-optic cables to get a better view and check for victims.

Then Harley searched a Hallmark store that was still in relatively good shape. As he rounded the corner beyond stacks of greeting cards, he stopped. Ahead of him was a dream come true. The wall was covered with stacks of his favorite toys, all bright and soft and ready to be chomped on.

He'd found Beanie Baby heaven. Harley somehow maintained his discipline but sat transfixed until Rob joined him, gave him a sympathetic pat, and informed him they couldn't remove merchandise. Rob also knew that was the end of the search as far as Harley was concerned; there was no way Harley could finish searching the store in the face of the Holy Grail of Beanie Babies. He called in a second dog to clear the rest of the store and walked a starstruck Harley out.

WITH THE MALL cleared by the dayshift, the nightshift was to focus on more of the collapsed underground areas. There was a subterranean vault beneath the WTC that housed gold and was supposedly strong enough to withstand the collapse. It was thought survivors might've sought shelter there. There were unknown numbers of other voids that might've served the same purpose. Nothing could be left unchecked.

Ana and Dusty, along with their firefighters, were summoned to an area near the Tower 2 collapse, where rescue workers had uncovered a deep void that turned into a tunnel. No one knew where it led or what it led to, so it was perfect for the search dogs. The two Goldens were excited for another day on the job. They practically pranced across the rubble to the edge of the void while the firefighters struggled to keep up. Rescue workers would stop what they were doing just to watch the dogs flow across the debris, not fully believing the skill of these animals.

The dogs and two rescue teams gathered at the opening of the tunnel. The floodlights of the crater barely pierced the yawning mouth of the void. Beyond the few feet of light, it was only darkness and the unknown. If anyone harbored claustrophobia, they did not show it.

Dusty and Randy and the first rescue team started down into the darkness. They soon disappeared from view. A tagline, a bright orange rope that allowed team members to find their way back out of the labyrinth, whipping back and forth against its anchor, was the only sign of the team from a minute before.

Ana and Rick waited their turn. The rescue squad leader and search specialist descended first, disappearing in the same manner as the first squad. There was a long wait, then the call for Rick and Ana came over the radio. They and the rest of the rescue squad made their way down into the tunnel. They picked their way carefully, trying to not let the crossing and swaying beams from flashlights fool their eyes. The cave-like opening quickly shrunk to the diameter of a large tunnel, and most of the humans could make it through only by crouching. There were small branches and voids heading off the main tunnel in different directions. Something caught Rick's eye in one of the smaller voids, something that seemed out of place. He held his flashlight on it for a better look. From between a stack of crushed debris hung a human leg, still wearing the pants of a suit and a business shoe. Rick radioed the surface for a human remains recovery team. He did his best to refocus himself after the unsettling sight, and led Ana onward.

Rick kept his flashlight on the tag line to make sure they stayed on course. Then came a four-foot drop onto an angled slab of concrete—some of the first intact concrete Rick had seen since arriving on Ground Zero. The team walked down the slab and found themselves in an underground parking area. They were brought to a temporary halt as recon elements scouted ahead. Rick sat down next to Ana, who'd propped herself against a support pillar. In front of him, a large steel beam pierced the ceiling like a giant arrowhead. The search team stared at it in a sort of frightened reverence, only imagining the ungodly amount of force required to push the beam through a full story of hardened earth.

FARTHER DOWN THE tunnel, Dusty and the first rescue team steadily gophered their way down deeper into the crushed depths. They didn't know where the passage ended. They searched everything they could along the way, following separated veins to dead ends. They went so deep that they lost radio contact with the surface, but continued forward. Their only company was the empty echoes of bootfalls and the slight jingle of Dusty's lead. Their headlamps would reach long fingers out into the dark in front of them, but the dust was a swirling and sparkling curtain that masked anything more than a couple yards down the tunnel. Soon their headlamps framed a large opening and the rescue team found themselves entering a subway terminal, almost four stories beneath the surface. There was no ambient light whatsoever. The rubble from the collapsed towers that had flooded the terminal made seeing anything at a distance almost impossible, even with flashlights. They would have to rely on Dusty's nose.

Randy followed Dusty around the subway's loading platform. The line ended in a complete collapse, but on the track opposite the platform was a subway car. It would need to be searched. Dusty made her way across the platform. Mid-stride, she suddenly sunk into the earth and disappeared from sight. Randy called out and rushed forward. His light caught Dusty's movement but she appeared to be . . . swimming? His light also revealed the loading platform by his feet cresting in small waves. It wasn't a platform at all. The mystery space was actually another railway track, but water from broken pipes had flooded the gap until it was full. The darkness had turned the space into an illusion, making it seem like a solid surface. Dusty, a little surprised, but undeterred, continued swimming toward the subway car, still wanting to search. Randy called her back and hoisted her out of the muck. There was probably fuel and oil and mud and ash and blood and no telling what else in that liquid. Sure enough, as Randy wiped and watered off his eager partner as best he could, the dark sheen remained. Dusty had been turned the color of pure black oil. She looked like she was now a longhaired Black Lab instead of a Golden.

Dusty was unfazed by the wardrobe change, and the team had a laugh, but knew they had to get her out immediately to decontamination. They quickly regrouped and started making their way back to the surface. Dusty tried to remedy the situation by rolling in a pile of ash in one of the burned-out hallways. It wasn't much of an improvement.

Even with the sludge, Dusty didn't slow a bit. Randy watched with pride as his new "Black Lab" continued to search the tunnels and voids as they returned to the surface. It didn't matter the circumstance, Dusty just wanted to do her job.

WHILE RANDY AND Dusty made their way back up to decontamination, Ana, Rick, and the rest of the other rescue team burrowed in a different direction through the parking structure. They made their way down a partially collapsed hallway. They hadn't heard from the first rescue squad, who were too deep for radios as well.

The hallway dead-ended, but a hole in the wall allowed forward progress to continue. Two of the team members investigated ahead and found more voids for Ana and Rick to search. They came to another hole in the floor. Ana would have to sit this one out as Rick had no idea where the hole led or what was at the bottom. He gave Ana's lead to his rescue squad teammate and began to worm his way down into the hole. It was barely large enough for him to fit, so tight his flashlight was ineffective and he had to feel the way with his feet. He probed until his boot found purchase and then repeated the process, slow and steady.

He pushed deeper, crawling on his belly as the walls shrank around him until he felt like the air he breathed was at hazard. Another small hole in the wall appeared at his side. When Rick illuminated it with his flashlight, he felt an electric chill ripple over his skin. What the flashlight revealed was surreal. Framed by the jagged edges of the hole was an underground office, fully intact. Chairs aligned, racks of metal filing cabinets, and a long desk with computers, all as it was, save a thin layer of dust. It was like nothing had ever happened and when the night was over, all the employees would return tomorrow for work at 9:00 a.m.

The hole into the office was smaller than anything he'd passed through up to that point, but it had to be checked, and Rick had to do it alone. He took a minute to compose himself, and then pushed forward into the hole. Immediately, he felt the wall grab his hips and shoulders. His progress halted. In that moment, the danger of what they were all doing gripped his mind. They were stories below the ground, beneath millions of tons of unstable rubble. They were too deep to communicate with the surface. They had run out of tag line long ago. Rick was alone, with only the darkness and the desperate heaves of his breath echoing off the stone and steel now holding him hostage. He could smell only the stale lime of concrete and dust. He could see only black. He did not know if he would be able to escape.

As quickly as the emotions seized him, another thought

brought things back into perspective. These were the same thoughts a trapped victim would be having. Worse, probably. If he were a victim, he'd be unable to move, probably injured, probably unable to breathe properly, unaware of any rescue effort. He'd have nothing to do except let the blood leave his body and the dust coat his lungs and wait for a slow death. This was why he was down here in the first place, why he knew he had to check this void regardless of the risks. With a final shove, Rick forced his body through the hole and into the office.

The office stared back at him, silent and dead. Rick scanned the area with his flashlight. The pristine office he'd seen framed through the hole quickly stopped short where the roof had completely collapsed. The stench of death hit him like a punch. He checked the small office area. There were people here, but nobody alive. Rick stood in silent shock for a moment.

"Are you all right?" a voice called from behind him. Rick's teammate had worked his way to the hole outside the office.

"Yes," Rick replied slowly. "I'm coming out."

Rick forced his way back through the hole and rejoined his teammate and Ana. It was then that he remembered the walls feeling too close and the burning urge to get out of this dark prison as quickly as possible. But he held it together and just focused on Ana as they made their way back.

They worked their way back up the tunnel, lifting Ana up the big drops until they reached the rest of the team.

Ana was still bursting with energy, but the rescue squad had been ordered back to the surface; they'd been down too long and things were getting even more dangerous.

Ana led the way back up to the surface. They learned the other rescue squad was also on their way back to the surface. After hours below ground, both teams finally emerged out onto the top of the rubble pile on the surface. They would've liked to see sunlight, but of course it was still the middle of the night.

The squads took a moment to collect themselves. Ana and Dusty were still itching to get going on the next search. The teams talked to some of the firefighters on the surface. Rick recalls being emotionally drained, but the hardest part was telling them that no one had been found alive and only being able to report the remains of the deceased in the office.

Rick said nothing about his ordeal getting into the collapsed office, or the actions of the rescue team that went well beyond the call of duty and any consideration of personal safety; the actions no one saw nor reported on the evening news; the actions for which they would receive no extra pay or special recognition; which they did simply out of a dedication to try to help other humans in a time of need.

Instead, everyone quietly made their way across the rubble pile, Ana and the midnight-oil-edition of Dusty leading the way, ready to do it all over again if the call came.

Twenty-six

REINFORCEMENTS

On September 19 Abby and Debra Tosch and the rest of the stranded teams finally made it to Ground Zero to begin their search with the second wave of FEMA task forces. Their arrival made thirteen SDF teams to deploy in total. The second wave had been receiving small reports of what the other teams were seeing on the pile, but those didn't provide much comfort. The general message was *There is only steel and it's like nothing anybody has ever seen or trained for.*

Even with the hectic route to deployment through San Diego, Abby was primed and ready to search. When Debra first led her onto the mountain of twisted steel, a sight that caused a searcher's stomach to tighten, Abby was elated to see a new job site and another chance to win her game. For Debra, the pressure was higher. She'd arrived at an area by the South Tower where a breathing apparatus from a firefighter had been uncovered. This late in the rescue effort, there was dim hope that anyone was still alive, but firefighters weren't about to let the possibility of recovering one of their own go unchecked. There were hundreds of them scouring the wreckage and delicately removing debris pieces by hand.

The FDNY battalion chief led Abby and Debra up a small rise until they were on an elevated ledge of crumpled steel. He briefed Debra on the location of the apparatus and where he needed searched. Then he called off the other firefighters. All of them. The firefighters slowly made their way off the pile and trudged past, their masked faces sullen beneath bright hardhats, their heavy overalls covered with dust. "We've found they search better when no one is around," the chief said after seeing Debra's surprise and then stepped back, allowing Abby to take center stage. Debra glanced behind her. A few companies' worth of firefighters now watched her and the empty pile in front of them. This was why she and Abby were here. She released the dog to search.

Abby was off without an inkling of apprehension about her new environment. If anything, she was attacking it with the vigor of the greatest game in the world. She moved over the steel like it was flat ground, easily adapting to the new terrain. She used the wide I beams as high walkways until they split or twisted awkwardly. Then she jumped onto another beam or down onto another flat slab of metal with a graceful ballerina landing. She skipped over small bundles of wire and rebar and skirted the knife-edged steel panels sticking out of the ground like misplaced street signs. Her nose went down, then up, then back down again. Hundreds of eyes watched and prayed. Abby was cruising like business as usual. She high-stepped over rusted pipes that bent and curled in and out of the debris like exposed tree roots. She covered the entire search area so fast, Debra ran her through again just to get some more of her energy out. Sadly though, Abby gave no indication there was anyone left alive. Debra called Abby back and praised her girl for an incredible job. That was the easy part. The difficult part would be the moment all the handlers had come to hate: telling the others there were no survivors.

Debra informed the chief of the search results. "Maybe we can bring in another dog and get different results," she added, trying to soften the blow.

The chief shook his head. "No," he said. "That was the most thorough dog I've ever seen." With that, the firefighters returned to the pile, moving faster and efficiently, their rescue effort now only a recovery.

It was heartbreaking for Debra, but anybody who'd watched the search knew with absolute certainty that if there had been victims still alive, Abby would have found them.

———

BILLY, ABBY'S RIVAL, was also among the second wave of dog teams to arrive. Normally paired with a handler from his San Diego Task Force, Billy's new partner was none other than Abby. Debra Tosh conferenced with Billy's handler, firefighter Mike Scott; they wondered if the friction between the dogs would affect their searching ability. At this point in the recovery effort, things were humming along, so they decided not to rock the boat.

Billy and Abby, on the other hand, seemed to sense the seriousness of the situation. They kept a lid on any angst they held for one another. They were both consummate professionals the whole time.

Billy searched the ground-level WTC plaza area first. The plaza area was treacherous, and bordered deep canyons of sharp steel, some five or six stories deep. The only thing still left intact was a twenty-five-foot-tall copper globe, a sculpture that stood between the two towers symbolizing world peace, now battered and dented, its top peeled open.

Unlike some of his counterparts, the dog who would squeeze through my fence after toys had a search style that was very deliberate. He would seem to check and then double-check everything in a methodical way instead of the harum-scarum manner of many of the other dogs. His pace on the pile was always measured and he seemed to meter his energy such that he could keep searching for hours.

ZACK, THE KEY-STEALING pup, arrived along with the second wave of task forces. Zack started off searching strong, but after the first day, "dad"-since-birth and handler Jeff Place noticed Zack acting a bit sluggish. There was a traveling Veterinary Medical Assistance Team (VMAT) on standby whenever dogs were searching, and one rolled up in a four-wheel-drive cart to examine the Chocolate Lab. He seemed fine, so the vet rehydrated him with fluids. That night, Zack rested quietly in his crate. The next morning, he was all-systems-go. A little stressed and a little dehydrated most likely, Zack overcame both easily and never looked back. He timed it perfectly, too. It was his eighth birthday.

DUKE'S ENTHUSIASM DIDN'T wane a bit when he and his handler, Howard Orr, came to their first search at Ground Zero. Duke did not see the sharp steel or towering piles of rubble, but an exciting new environment he could conquer! Duke's ability to throw caution to the wind made him a force of nature when he was searching. Nothing slowed him. Howard remembers one search where Duke stopped on a dime to investigate a smell. The big Lab shoved his head deep into a hole. His head completely submerged, Duke's rear paws were casually propped up on a half-inch piece of rebar. Just another day at the office.

Duke's main search area was focused on the plaza in the center of the WTC complex. Early on, there was a void near the entrance to the plaza. Duke, though not alerting, was showing interest. Howard informed some of the rescuers. His comments were initially met with skepticism. The area Duke was pointing out was the entrance to this particular search area and there'd been close to a thousand rescue workers traveling over the same spot without noticing a thing. But they took the energetic Lab seriously and committed a recovery team to the spot. By the next day, they had extracted the remains of three fallen firefighters. Three more families that would get closure thanks to Duke.

The find brought Howard Orr to a crossroads. Duke was not trained to alert on cadavers or human remains, but he seemed willing to do so. Search dogs can be cross-trained on multiple disciplines, but not on the fly. If you try to force a dog into a mold they don't know, it can sometimes break them completely. It's a lot like running a car on a different type of fuel—it might work for a while, but eventually you're going to have engine problems. Duke and most of the SDF dogs were resilient, but if they were pushed too far, they would have to be retrained in their primary field of live find, and no longer be useful at Ground Zero. It would be a fine line to walk.

Howard remembers rescuers lining up with places for Duke to search. Duke went through about five searches when Howard noticed his gung-ho boy was stopping every few minutes to look back at him, like he needed reassurance. Duke was getting confused. Having trained so long with him, Howard knew the signs immediately and pulled him off the pile. They were done. Pushing Duke any more would be counterproductive. Everyone understood, and didn't want to lose Duke as a live-search asset, so they thanked the big Lab for what he'd found already.

Abby, who'd been searching up a storm and doing Mama Murphy proud, had a similar experience finding human remains. She would slow and sniff an area, just for a second. Her pause was often so quick, Debra would've missed it if she wasn't watching Abby the entire time. But she caught it and on one search they were able to mark four different sites for human remains. That was four families that would receive peace. Many of the other teams had similar experiences. Even though the SDF dogs were not trained to find human remains, the teams were happy to contribute in any manner they could.

MANNY, THE NEUROTIC Border Collie, and handler Ron Weckbacher began the night shift with the second wave of task forces. Ron shared everyone else's sentiments when he first viewed the smoking and backlit rubble pile. It was beyond comprehension. He wasn't sure how Manny would be able to handle it.

They began to traverse across the steelscape for Manny's

first search. Ron clipped Manny onto a long lead and then looked down to check his footing. He reminded himself to stay as positive as possible—Border Collies especially pick up on their handlers' emotions and would interpret anything negative as a problem with their search. When he looked up, Manny was already gone, blazing his way out front, sharp ears up like two black diamonds, ready to get to business.

Ron was with Manny on the rubble pile when one of the FDNY firefighters beckoned him over near the corner of where the tower once stood. The firefighter pointed a gloved finger toward some slabs of steel and debris. "My buddy was right here," he said. "The last I saw him was right here." Ron had Manny search the area. He knew the chances of finding anyone alive, as did the sweat-and-soot-soaked firefighter in front of him, but they would search anyway.

Manny searched expertly as normal, the small area only taking him a matter of minutes, but made no indication or alert. Ron called him off. "I'm sorry," he told the fire-fighter. "My dog isn't giving any indication of live scent." Ron watched the light in the firefighter's eyes dim as the small amount of hope melted away. I knew from experience there is nothing that can prepare you to be the messenger of this news, and no way you will ever forget it.

———

ON THE HOME front in Ojai, the next obstacle to raise its head was our shortage of volunteers. Time had lost all meaning to me; island time in the condo had morphed into perpetual daytime as I fielded requests for interviews, delegated tasks to volunteers, and kept up on the progress from our teams in the field. I was a general of sorts, and we were in the thick of a pitched battle. We had other volunteers bring in meals and walk dogs (our staff was always encouraged to bring in their family pets). The volunteers had pushed through like good soldiers for as long as possible, but they had families and jobs and lives to attend to. Still, we couldn't stop the fight mid-battle. There were too many people counting on us. When the cry went up among the ranks that the volunteers needed relief, I had to think quickly.

"Nobody goes home until they have a replacement," I told them.

Underwhelmed silence.

"Call a friend," I continued. "A friend or a neighbor, or a relative. Once you get a replacement, that's your ticket home."

That's how we kept our train rolling along. Volunteers could be trained quickly to answer phones or write thank-you notes. Hell, they didn't even need to know what we were doing, we just needed to keep doing it.

Twenty-seven

"WHERE CAN I GET DOGS LIKE THAT?"

When the handlers brought their dogs back from a search shift, their day didn't end. There was always a veterinary check-in in case the dogs had received any injuries on the rubble pile. Then the vet would irrigate the dog's eyes and nose to help clear the dust. Then it would be up to the handlers to clean off the dogs completely. In cases like the Exxon Valdez, Randy was scrubbing his dog for hours. Most dogs, as you would expect, were less than thrilled to get the scrub-down. Billy, the skinny and thoughtful Black Lab, however, loved it. A pup of refined taste, or perhaps he was just going back to his Labrador penchant for the water, Billy would relish each decon bath like it was his day at the spa.

Most of the time after searches, the dogs weren't even tired. Rick remembers Ana bouncing off the walls when everybody else was ready for sleep. They would often need to be exercised again before being crated for bed. Only once the dog was completely taken care of and bedded down could the weary firefighters stuff some food in their mouths and stumble off to their cots for a few hours of sleep, their fellow dogless firefighters already hours into slumber. Then the handlers would be the first up in order to get their dogs prepped for the day. Twelve-hour shifts at Ground Zero easily stretched into seventeen hours awake and active.

Most of the handlers don't recall fatigue having an effect on them or their attitude. They took solace in talking with and helping out the FDNY and other rescuers, reading support letters from home, or simply taking in the enormous outpouring of positive energy from across the globe. Celebrities stopped by the BOO to show their support for the rescue effort, and of course no one could miss out on petting the dogs. Dusty made fast friends with Chevy Chase, Mayor Rudy Giuliani, and numerous senators and congressmen. One evening, the rescuers were called forward and lined up as President George W. Bush came by to pay his respects and thank the rescue workers. The president made his way down the line and reached Dusty first. He started giving her a good ear-scratching. Ana, who doesn't like to be second in anything, immediately got jealous and lunged forward to get her share of attention. Her enthusiastic charge shoved Dusty out of the way and rammed the president right between the legs. You have to respect a lady of action, and, fortunately, the Secret Service did not tackle her. The president laughed it off and gave both dogs an equal share of attention.

During the long days and nights, the handlers also took energy from their dogs. The SDF dogs never seemed to tire. Even after fourteen days of searching some of the most difficult rubble on earth, our dogs were so excited to do their jobs they were pulling their handlers to the pile in the morning.

Word about our dogs' ability started getting around. Dusty and Ana were called to an urgent search on what was now being called "the pit"—the deep crater where Tower 2, the South Tower, had collapsed. This was the area where most firefighters were believed to be buried. When Rick and Randy arrived with the dogs, they saw long lines of firefighters and police and some civilians stretched across the rubble pile. They were again resorting to an old-fashioned bucket brigade. They would fill five-gallon buckets with as much rubble as possible then hand them down the line.

The terrain in the search area was so unforgiving, the dogs from another task force were too exhausted to search and the FDNY battalion chief doubted any canine would be able to handle it. Rick and Randy surveyed the area and informed the chief it would be no problem for the SDF dogs.

The bucket brigades were put on hold as Randy prepped Dusty and then unleashed her to search. The skeptical chief watched as Dusty negotiated the rubble just like she'd been trained. Pluis would've been proud. Soon, Dusty was out of audio range to hear verbal commands, so Randy switched to whistle blows and hand signals. He sent his diligent partner across the pile with a quick blow on the whistle and a flick of his hand. Suddenly, Dusty stopped and began an alert bark. From behind a distant mound of rubble, a firefighter emerged—it was a rescue worker who hadn't heard the command to clear the pile. Everyone was disappointed it wasn't a live find, but there was no doubt about the SDF dogs' capabilities. Dusty finished searching the area. Near one side of the pile, she paused, almost like she was going to alert, then she lifted one paw, paused again, and turned away. Randy, who'd studied Dusty's body language over hundreds of searches, had never seen this particular one and was a little perplexed by it. It was as if she wanted to alert on a victim, but at the same time, knew she shouldn't. Then he put it together. There were human remains buried there. Just like Abby and Duke, Dusty and many of the SDF dogs helped find human remains in the rubble. Even if they weren't live finds, they were still contributing to the search effort and helping bring down some of the missing persons posters that hung in the alleyway.

Randy had the spot marked, and called Dusty off the rubble pile. She came trotting back through the steepled rubble with the same ease she'd embarked on her search. Behind him, Randy heard the FDNY battalion chief become a believer. "Where do I get dogs like that?" he asked the search team leader.

WHEN THEY WEREN'T searching, the dogs became the face of relief for the other rescue workers. They were the unofficial therapy dogs of Ground Zero. When you traverse a landscape of destruction for twelve hours a day, where everything wants to cut you and a misstep could mean serious injury, a soft, warm creature is a welcome sight. When your daily mission involves scouring destruction trying to find anybody alive, a friendly snout and a soul who will do nothing but sit by your side is more powerful than any medicine. The dogs provided hope and a return to normalcy.

Debra Tosh remembers sitting with Abby at a staging area between searches. An NYFD firefighter approached her. His face was powdered black with soot and striped with lines of sweat. He asked Debra if he could pet her dog. Debra said of course. Without another word, the firefighter slumped down next to Abby, buried his face in her black fur, and wept. Young Abby sat with the firefighter, wagging her tail and happy to sit as long as needed. After a while the firefighter raised his head and composed himself. To completely get over what he was going through would take a lifetime, but he did look a little better. "That's exactly what I needed," he said and returned to work.

Duke was always one-track minded, so when a group of firefighters approached Howard Orr to pet the big Lab, Howard was dubious. He didn't want to break his dog's concentration, but here was a group of guys who'd been away from home and were pretty much sleeping on the pile. They needed some relief. Howard agreed and Duke soaked up the attention. Once they were done petting Duke, he shifted gears right back into search mode and powered on. It became a nightly ritual for the exhausted firefighters, and Howard (and Duke) were glad they could help any way they could.

There were numerous other instances where the dogs provided comfort to those in need. After searches, firefighters on the pile would gather around the dogs and give congratulatory pats and ear scratches. Just watching the dogs flow across the rubble with such enthusiasm helped raise spirits. The dogs' happy faces every morning, ready to work, made the job for everyone else that much easier. In an environment so harsh over such a long duration, every little piece of morale is crucial. The attention was great for the dogs as well. They loved their newfound fame and used it as their fuel to go out every day and conquer.

———

ALMOST A WEEK into the rescue effort, the SDF hit the mainstream news for the first time. If we'd known what we were doing, we'd have had our name out much earlier, but we weren't some marketing agency. We dealt in dogs, that's it.

Every media outlet had taken on volunteers and temporary workers to deal with the 9/11 coverage, and a temporary worker from Fox called me one morning.

"This is such important work you do," she said. "This should be nationally known."

By this point I'd lost track of how many interviews I'd done and wasn't exactly caught up on my sleep so, a little incredulously, I asked, "And just how do I do that?"

The woman had no answer, but said it was a shame our information wasn't out there.

The next morning, we noticed a distinct uptick in phone calls from the East Coast. Normally, we'd receive a smattering of calls from all across the country, so we were about to write this off as a fluke, but then, an hour later, there was an uptick in calls from the Midwest. We didn't know what was happening, but we knew then it was not a fluke.

I turned on the news in our office. We watched and waited as the news anchors ran through continuing coverage of the 9/11 recovery efforts. Then, in the crawling ticker on the bottom of the screen on Fox was the SDF's mission statement and our contact information. It would scroll through every so often on a given time interval.

Because of the time zones, people on the East Coast saw it as they awoke, and now the Midwest was starting to see it. It was the first time we'd had our name on such a public and nationally distributed stage. The word would continue to spread as people across the country awoke and turned on the news.

I reached out to my small squad of bleary-eyed volunteers. "Nobody goes home!" I said cheerfully.

The next day, we started taking calls from the East Coast again in the early morning and the pattern continued throughout the day. Support was pouring in. I knew the information on the news ticker was refreshed often and had a short shelf life. We needed that information to stay up longer, so I called Fox and tracked down the temp worker who'd managed to get our information up in the first place.

"How long can our information stay up?" I asked. She answered her instructions were to remove it that day.

"Oh no," I said. "Just one more day. It's *really* important."

There was a long pause on the phone and then she admitted she could lose her instructions for one more day, but that was it.

"Do what you can!" I said and gave her my sincere thanks.

The SDF information remained on the crawler for another day. We didn't know it just yet, but that extra day had a tremendous impact on the future of the foundation.

I never talked to the Fox temp worker again, nor did I get her full name. But may she live forever and all of her days be filled with the utmost happiness.

AFTER ONE LONG search on September 19, as Dusty soaked in her decon bath, the public relations coordinator of the task force approached Randy. He asked if Dusty would want to head over to Wall Street to close the New York Stock Exchange. Randy had been awake for almost sixteen hours. He wasn't a big fan of publicity stunts. But this was supposed to be an honor, and he knew it would help spread the word about what the task force was doing. Randy agreed and finished bathing Dusty so she could get ready for the big ball.

A few minutes later, Dusty, spruced and brushed, accompanied Randy to lower Manhattan, only a few blocks from the rubble of the WTC. The NYSE had reopened on September 17 and, being so close to the destruction at Ground Zero, was thus viewed as a victory in itself.

After a quick briefing and photo op, Dusty strutted out onto a platform overlooking the trading floor along with a number of other first responders. The floor was crammed with the large TV monitors covered with colorful charts and graphs. The many traders milled about. A few reporters worked on segments with their camera crews. Dusty, Randy, and other rescue workers from the task force gathered around the closing bell. Dusty, the young pup who used to hug me around the waist because she distrusted what might happen in the next minute of her life, ascended a small stool so she was front and center, looking out over the center of commerce for the United States.

They waited for the clock to hit 4:00 p.m. and then got the signal. Randy gave a shake command and Dusty pawed the button and the bell started ringing. The cheers of everyone roared throughout the hall. The market was closed. The applause continued. Dusty was happy to sit on the stool and soak it in.

"Has any other dog ever done this?" Randy asked one of the NYSE staff.

"We had the Taco Bell dog do a promotional thing once," the man replied.

Randy looked at Dusty, who was still relishing the applause. Less than an hour ago she'd been traversing shattered steel, covered in the dust and grime from collapsed buildings. Now she was calm and composed and happy.

Randy shook his head. "That's not a real dog," he said. "Dusty is the first real dog to do this."

No one disagreed.

AS THE SECOND week of the rescue effort matured into a recovery effort—meaning the mission would focus more on recovering human remains as opposed to finding an unlikely live victim—the search teams were pushed out to the offices immediately surrounding Ground Zero.

These buildings had sustained damage and though they didn't collapse, might still have people trapped inside. It was a highly unlikely scenario, but the rescuers would leave no stone unturned. These locations were easier to search in terms of rubble as they only presented minor debris for the dogs to deal with. The problem though, was much more artificial. The majority of offices, especially the subterranean ones, had locked doors, some made of metal. Some of these buildings had almost a hundred floors, each packed with rows of locked offices. Breaking in and checking each office would be a monumental undertaking. Fortunately, the search dogs provided a shortcut.

The firefighters found as long as they could wedge the door open a crack, just enough to let scent escape, the dogs could verify if there was anybody inside. This expedited the office searches exponentially and prevented even more property damage to buildings that had already endured so much.

During one of the searches, Ana and Rick climbed their way to the top of a darkened bank building on Church Street that faced Ground Zero. One of the offices they searched was open. The office was empty and undamaged except for the west-facing window. The glass was coated with a thick layer of dust that gave the appearance of a dirty window shade. Its center had been pierced by a piece of flying debris leaving a bullet-shaped hole and spider-webbed glass. Light from Ground Zero spilled through the tiny hole. Rick put his eye up to the hole and looked out. For the first time, he was able to see the entirety of Ground Zero. The devastation seemed to stretch on forever into the night. Directly below him was the major rubble pile. Floodlights bathed the debris in a pallid glow as steam rose from crevices like ghosts rising from graves. Hundreds of rescue workers shoveled, hauled, and searched, tirelessly and feverishly. It was the American spirit in action—when darkness and destruction descends upon us, we turn on a light and get to work.

THE DOGS AND handlers from the initial wave of FEMA task forces, along with our pilot program dogs, returned home to a massive welcome. They were mobbed with media and supporters when they landed at Travis Air Force Base in California. After so many days on an isolated disaster site, it was a little overwhelming. The media is immediately attracted to dogs, so many of the handlers had to put on their happy face and say a few words for the cameras. They tried to remind themselves that the majority of people out there just wanted the rescuers to know they supported and appreciated their service.

But it was—and always will be—difficult. When you see only destruction for weeks at a time, nobody feels like a hero. On the pile, there is only dust and grit and death. Those memories are permanent. While everyone else has the luxury of voicing support and moving on, the things our first responders see will live in their minds forever.

For the dogs, it might have been just a game, but they gave it their all. Every single one of our dogs had left not a single ounce of fuel in the tank. As they finally rejoined the families of their handlers, they took the cue to rest.

Harley in particular enjoyed his time off. The big guy slept for days, no doubt comforted by dreams of Beanie Baby heaven.

Twenty-eight

AMERICAN MADE

As the initial wave of California task forces began to return home, I also made it back to Ojai and was dealing with the aftermath of the two-week run for the foundation. Donations were still coming in nonstop. We still didn't have an adequate computer system set up, so we kept track of things the old-fashioned way, on paper. I'd brought in a futon so I could nap between phone calls that stretched late into the night. Nobody was even paying attention to how much we were raising. We were just trying to keep up with writing the thank-you notes. Eventually, I got around to asking our volunteer in charge of financial deposits how much we'd raised.

"Fifty-six thousand dollars."

Wow. Fifty-six thousand dollars in a week? I could hardly believe it. Here was this little peanut organization used to bringing in a couple hundred per fundraiser and now we'd raised thousands. "You're telling me we raised fifty-six thousand dollars this week?" I asked, more excited than actually clarifying.

The volunteer gave me an exasperated look. "That's just this morning, Wilma," she said. "We raised fifty-six thousand dollars this morning."

I was speechless. When we finally totaled the final number, the end result was staggering. With donations of $50 or so at a time, we'd raised over one million dollars (equating to approximately $1.4 million in 2019). One million dollars raised meant around twenty thousand Americans had donated their own money to support us. That was twenty thousand people who believed their money could help build the next chapter of the SDF. Everyone was ecstatic, but we weren't about to celebrate. Now it was up to us to follow through on our promise. There could be no slipups from here on out.

AS THE FIRST week of October came to a close, Abby and Debra Tosch and the rest of the wave-two task forces packed up their things and boarded a bus back to McGuire Air Force Base. Everyone was exhausted. They had pushed their abilities and endurance to the absolute limit.

As the group of rescuers sat in a large grass field at the

airfield waiting for their flights, Debra and the other handlers pulled the dogs out of their crates. They released the leashes but gave no commands. The dogs needed no direction. They knew this was free play. The dogs that gave it all on the rubble, now gave it all again. But here there were no rules. Abby sprinted and darted through the pack growing ever wilder. Duke charged everything in sight, resulting in more than a few body slams. Manny, ever the diligent Border Collie, skirted the outside of the melee, doing his best to bring order to this unwieldy herd. Then Duke broke from the pack and found the only mud puddle on the entire airbase and launched himself into it. He was over the moon as he paraded his new extra chocolate coating around the other clean dogs.

The handlers watched on with pure delight. For the first time in two weeks, they could sit on even ground and breathe easy. They looked around to realize that more people had joined the audience. Soon the entire task force was there, laughing at the wild rumpus and enjoying the catharsis the show provided. For all they'd been through, it was nice to simply bask in the unbridled glow of dogs being dogs.

FOR PLUIS, THEIR performance was a testament to her training—it was clear she'd shaped a wild pack of rejects and misfits into some of the best search dogs in the world. There wasn't a soul who saw our dogs work that doubted their tenacity and ability. There wasn't a soul that, if the roles were reversed and they were below that rubble, wouldn't want those dogs coming for them.

I really never doubted the ability of the dogs, or our trainers, volunteers, or anyone associated with the SDF. But to provide a helping paw when our nation needed it most was an honor. With the generous funding coming in, I knew my unspoken goal of 168 teams wasn't just a daydream anymore. I also knew it was just a matter of time before the nation called on us again. The SDF needed to be ready.

And we would need more dogs.

PART III

Twenty-nine

LEFT FOR DEAD

Next to the southbound railroad tracks near Fresno, California, a Yellow Lab whose coat was the color of polished brass writhed in the dirt and brown crabgrass, clawing at his face. He didn't know why his nose and eyes burned. When he batted his snout, his paws burned too. He tried to get away from this place he didn't know and that rumbled with large machines. Perhaps he would be able to escape across the industrial landscape and find some scraps among the collection of fast food joints or the mobile homes that bordered the highway nearby. Maybe he could find his way home. He knew he had done something wrong, but he didn't understand what. He tried to squirm away, but his tugs were stopped short, as a piece of rope, tied to the steel of the railroad track, dug into his neck.

The young Lab had a tremendous reservoir of energy, which had probably got him in trouble in the first place. When his so-called owners found it too much to handle, they'd lashed the pup to a railroad track and left him to die. The abandonment not being enough to quench the owner's sadistic psyche, this person had sprayed the defenseless puppy with mace. Unable to see, smell, or escape the train tracks, the puppy wouldn't survive the day.

BUT THE YOUNG Lab had fight. He survived long enough for a good Samaritan to spot and report him. He eventually landed in a local animal shelter. His wounds were given basic treatment and his starved and dehydrated body finally got some nourishment. He still was suffering the aftereffects from the pepper spray, and since the shelter had no other name, they dubbed him Mace.

Out of the frying pan and into the fire. Mace's rescue from the railroad tracks was only a short reprieve. The shelter he'd been put in was a high-kill shelter. They did not have the resources to house another dog, especially one with medical needs. Despite obvious abuse and injuries, Mace's roiling energy made it unlikely anyone would adopt him. The shelter had to make the tough call. For the second time in as many days, the young Lab was given a death sentence.

———

AS THE EUTHANASIA-HOUR approached, the shelter employees searched for a home for Mace. It would be a tough
fit. Mace was a handsome dog, but the pepper spray and
his rough condition had left him not looking his best. No
one knew what type of physical scars he would bear from
the incident and a puppyhood of abuse. Mace would also
be a big dog with an abundance of energy—another strike
against him. With so many other animals needing a home,
there wasn't much the employees could do to further the
dog's case. All their attempts to find even a temporary
home fell short. Mace, still recovering from his ordeal, entered into what might be the last hour of his life.

THEN THE SHELTER employees made a heads-up play.
They had heard the SDF was looking for high-drive dogs
and figured if Mace could survive what he did, he probably could do anything. The shelter contacted firefighter
Jeff Place, Zack's handler, and pleaded Mace's case. Jeff immediately agreed to rescue Mace. With less than an hour
until he was scheduled to receive the needle, Mace was
given a third chance at life.

IT DIDN'T TAKE Mace long to recover from his injuries. He
tested off the charts for prey drive and nobody needed to

ask the question if he was physically tough enough to be a search dog. His face, once cringed with pain and injury, smoothed. His eyes widened into kind, almond ovals. The muscles in his shoulders and hips fleshed out and angled into sharp slabs. Mace looked like he'd been carved from marble. He wasn't just a good-looking dog; he was cover-model handsome. We all knew the last tie to his rough puppyhood had to be cut—it no longer fit the proud and confident dog who now sat before us. Without any second thoughts, Mace became Ace, and left for Sundowners to start his training with Pluis.

Thirty

FIRE AND ICE

Around the same time Ace was awaiting training, the SDF received another handsome Yellow Lab, although this pup's background was much easier on the emotions. The Lab was a purebred with high drive and plenty of horsepower, donated by a breeder who'd wanted to contribute to the SDF.

His coat was more platinum than yellow and shined like a translucent crystal in the sun. His name, Ice, couldn't have been more fitting. With muscle cut into sharp angles, the dog looked like an ice sculpture, and acted just as cool. Confidence is great for a search dog, but the flipside is that it can give a dog a mind of his own and an I-do-what-I-want attitude. Perhaps that's a bit of an understatement in

Ice's case. Needless to say, his future handler would have his hands full.

It wasn't long after Ice entered the SDF ranks that I got a call from a New York firefighter. He was part of the FDNY hockey team, and his friend and teammate, Timmy McSweeney, had been killed in the line of duty on 9/11. Because of our service responding to the WTC attacks, and our preparation to respond to any other future disasters, the firefighter thought our foundation would be the best way to honor and carry on his friend's legacy of selfless service. He requested that the SDF name a dog after Timmy's FDNY Ladder Company, Recon. I couldn't think of a better match than our newly inherited Ice, so I agreed, and Ice became Recon. With the banner of FDNY now backing him, Recon left to start his training with Ace.

As Pluis started training the new class of recruits, she uncovered some issues with Ace, our lionhearted Yellow Lab. He startled easily. Any surprises were a no-no. Also, as one might expect from a dog so badly abused, strangers alarmed him. If you tried to touch him from behind, he would nip at your hand.

The good news was that on the rubble pile, all the strangers are hidden. Ace was dependable when it came time to search. He had the iron physicality that made tough terrain easy. He faced everything with the characteristic Labrador blue-collar view: *I've got a job and I'm gonna get it done.* He passed the search curriculum with flying colors.

He just needed some more confidence when it came to his downtime.

Pluis started adding more structure into Ace's routine where most of the other dogs would be allowed to relax—something as basic as a down-stay instead of simply releasing the dog after a search. The small rules helped keep Ace grounded. His behavior off the rubble pile would be a long game though, and he would need to be paired with a veteran handler who continued his structured routines. It took a little longer than average, but as he had done all his life, Ace adapted and overcame his handicaps, and graduated from training.

RECON, THE UNTAMABLE platinum Lab, had a slightly different issue. When he was on-task he was unshakable. When he was off-task, he was redefining the term wild.

There was a laundry list of things that distracted the dog—squirrels, rodents, birds, falling leaves, just about anything that moved. Actually, getting Recon from point A to point B was a challenge. Pluis had the duty of redirecting the runaway train every time he got off course. Not an easy task, but she discovered that as long as Recon could get the call of the wild out of his system every once in a while, he seemed to do fine. Soon, Recon too was ready to graduate.

When it came time to pair Recon with his handler, Pluis had a good candidate in mind, but she needed to confirm her feeling. She let Recon enter the pairing field in a full wild-horse gallop. Lined up in the enclosure with a few other firefighters waited Marin County Fire Captain Jim Boggeri.

At first, Recon paid the firefighters little mind, instead opting to sprint circles around the entire enclosure, a platinum streak across the green grass. It was clear whoever inherited this pup would need both a strong dedication to the job as well as a lighter side when the job was done in order to deal with Recon's jubilant goofiness. Jim took one look at this blitzing maniac of a dog and knew they were destined for each other.

Recon wanted to put these mortals to the test, though. He turned his focus to the firefighters and charged with no intention of stopping. Recon was a solid seventy pounds of this-is-my-world-you're-just-living-in-it and traveling at roughly the speed of light; he appeared to be intent on wiping all three firefighters off the map. One firefighter stepped out of the line of fire. A second flinched. Jim recognized the game of chicken Recon was playing and called the Lab's bluff. He stepped forward. Recon screeched to a halt just in time. The dog was ecstatic. He knew he'd found his handler.

Pluis thought the same thing. Every day was a combination of Friday and Christmas to Recon, and Jim had the high-spirited personality to manage such a dog. The pair started training together and bonded immediately. But Jim would soon find it would take more than a figurative handshake to quiet the dog's inner wild thing.

WHEN IT CAME to searching, Jim felt he had a lot of ground to make up before he was actually on equal footing with Recon. He was a horse cart trying to keep up with a Ferrari. Recon did not make things easy. He was a dog with a strong will. Rough and built to brawl, Recon did not need to be coddled or built up. When he stepped onto a rubble pile, it was his show, his way. If a search was not up to his speed, he would get bored. Unlike Abby, who would resort to playing tricks on rookie handlers, Recon would fly the dog equivalent of the middle finger, quit for the day, and go in search of better uses of his energy than the silly search game. Jim found himself constantly adjusting and accelerating his training in order to keep his dog engaged instead of blasting off on wild-goose chases. Literally.

Recon had an enormous prey drive, and his hunting lineage would spark immediate chases after any bird or rodent unfortunate enough to be around the pile when he was off his leash. It was a problem that would have to be solved before Recon could get FEMA certified.

Recon's modus operandi did not help the issue either. He followed in the footsteps of other Labs like Sherman and Duke in the sense that if the key did not fit, he just pushed harder. He would cover rubble piles as fast as possible in a scorched earth style of searching without regard for his own safety. During his initial FEMA test, Recon strained a muscle in his leg and Jim had to withdraw. In another training search, Recon stepped on a nail that went completely through his paw, but the dog still wanted to continue to search. During yet another certification test, Recon was finding the victims easily but would not start his bark alert. Unbeknownst to Jim, he had a ruptured eardrum and barking would cause excruciating pain. Eventually, Recon's drive trumped his pain and he alerted, but Jim found the injury and pulled him out. Once again, Recon was willing but Jim had to put on the brakes to avoid him driving until the wheels fell off. Recon didn't like brakes.

Jim grew frustrated. The dog had so much obvious potential, and yet Jim was unable to direct it. What made matters worse was that Jim was taking flak from the civilians outside the foundation in his training group. Perhaps they were frustrated by their own failures—many had been training their own dogs for years and still lacked certification. Whatever the case, Jim often became the target of the all-too-familiar angst nearly every person in the SDF had experienced by this point. They made jabs about his SAR skills, and whispered behind his back, slowly chipping away at his confidence as a handler. He would leave training sessions questioning whether he should even be there. He had felt such a connection with Recon, but maybe the dog would be better off with someone else.

I knew the feeling. I had experienced the same thing. The whole SDF team had. But Jim's fellow firefighters stepped up. The Three Rs from the pilot program—Rick, Randy, and Rob—continued to encourage and coach Jim. When Jim returned to Sundowners for more training, Pluis would assure him he was progressing and exactly the handler Recon needed.

The cycle continued. Jim would be broken down by the civilians, the firefighters and the SDF team would help weave together the frayed strands, and Jim and Recon would come back stronger. Recon started responding better. There was no watershed moment, only day after day of hard work. Soon, their teamwork was seamless.

JIM AND RECON had the privilege of traveling to New York and meeting with the family and teammates of fallen firefighter Tim McSweeney, whom Recon was named for. They saw the home station of Ladder 3. They talked with other firefighters who'd known Tim, and were now honored to see his legacy carried on by Recon. Jim recalls it as "one of the most influential, moving moments in my life, knowing that [as a firefighter] my fate could have been the same as Tim's." As Jim soaked in the warm reception of Tim's family and fellow firefighters, he silently vowed to honor Tim's legacy through his steadfast commitment in his work with Recon.

Recon and Jim would also receive another honor. In April 2005, a Chicago paramedic turned police officer named Steven Zourkas was killed in the line of duty. To honor his memory, the local department and community raised money for a memorial fund. Steven was always committed to helping others, so his family wanted to donate the money to a cause that would help carry on his legacy. They chose to sponsor a search dog, and Steven's two children chose Recon. Honored to be even considered, Jim and Recon continued their dedication to the job, their sponsors an everyday reminder of how much America's first responders sacrifice, and how they needed to continue living by such an example.

AS RECON AND Jim continued to climb, their newfound success presented one major problem for Recon: it was often boring. Sometimes he needed to spice things up. Nobody knew which breed of ancient wolves ran through Recon's veins but the universal consensus was that it was a rowdy bunch that still sometimes called to the big Lab, which usually occurred at the most inopportune times for his handler.

At one of our IronDog training camps, Recon and Jim had been doing exceptionally well throughout the various training scenarios. Their progress was showing and all in observance could see they were well on their way to FEMA certification. Then came the live-distractions test, which consisted of caged, live animals sprinkled among the rubble pile. A rabbit meditated quietly in one cage at the right side of the debris. A gaggle of chickens pecked around another cage on the left side of the debris. Both cages were in plain view of any dog approaching the pile. Their existence was solely to distract the dogs.

As Recon and Jim approached the pile, the distraction seemed to be working. Recon was straining against his lead, foaming at the mouth, ready to make some fresh chicken-rabbit soup.

"Ok, Jim?" Pluis, who was one of the judges for the search, asked skeptically.

Jim assured her Recon would be good as soon as he started searching. Pluis shrugged. Jim dropped the leash. Searching never even crossed Recon's mind. He charged the rabbit cage. He hit the cage at approximately the speed of sound and sent it flying—the entire cage—a good ten yards.

After the judges and handlers who weren't on the ground laughing recovered and righted the cage with an unhurt-but-probably-traumatized rabbit, Jim got Recon under control and reset to start the search again. Pluis mentioned Recon still seemed to have the warpath gleam in his eye. Jim again assured her Recon would have no problem this go-round. The rabbit looked on, eyes dilated into giant ovals that nearly swallowed its entire face. Jim dropped the leash. The rabbit no doubt breathed a sigh of relief because Recon charged in the completely opposite direction. The chickens this time caught the impact of the Yellow Lab missile.

Jim collected Recon again. No animals had been harmed, but he and Recon had some work to do. The act was great for comic relief, but not for a serious search. Recon would need to completely ignore any live animals if he was going to get his FEMA certification and be taken on a real disaster search.

Every dog has his or her weakness. Every SDF handler before him had faced similar issues. Even ringers like Ana and Abby had rough edges their handlers had to smooth out. Just like how they'd persevered through their previous training, Jim did not accept Recon's weakness as a permanent condition. He used his firefighter ingenuity and addressed the problem directly—he built a pigeon coup in his backyard. For a solid week after, Recon was enamored, ready to spring on any bird silly enough to shed the confines of the cage. Fortunately, none did, and soon, the novelty wore off for Recon. Birds and other creatures soon became no big deal. Recon could ignore them on the pile. When Recon and Jim showed up for the next IronDog, Recon didn't even blink at the live distractions. He was totally focused on the search.

Of course Recon was not one to leave us without a show. At the end of the IronDog training came the newly minted competition event. This portion of the event also allowed spectators and sponsors to come watch the dogs perform under pressure. One of the main events, and a fan favorite, was the speed-agility course where the dogs would compete for the fastest time. Next to the course, behind the spectators, was a large lake.

As Jim prepped for the course, Recon was entranced with the lake. Flocking in the water was a type of waterfowl he'd never seen before. They were round and neon green and bite-size. Jim, focusing on the course, didn't think the other handlers throwing tennis balls for their dogs into the lake would distract Recon.

Wrong.

The timer for the course started and Jim released Recon. Recon immediately veered to the side, splitting the crowd of spectators down the middle and sprinting straight into the lake. The timer for the course continued to run. As he'd done so often, Jim gathered a now soaking and ecstatic Recon back through the chuckling crowd to restart the course. The timer was still running. His call of the wild answered, Recon was now ready to do the boring agility work. This time when Jim dropped his leash Recon stayed on course, clicking off obstacle after obstacle with his usual foolhardy speed. Recon crossed the finish line and the timer stopped. Even with the detour to the lake, Recon had finished in the fastest time of the day.

Like the live animals, Jim would have to go on to desensitize Recon to the lure of tennis balls. In this case though, he didn't plan on building a backyard tennis court.

Thirty-one

BROKEN BEYOND REPAIR

On the surface, Cody was a perfect pet. The young Golden Retriever was Christmas-card friendly, quick with a lick to the face, and handsome. He had a slender build and a long, thin snout that looked like he could thread it through the eye of a needle. He always seemed to be wearing a beaming dog smile. But beneath the surface was a much different dog, one who didn't want to stay cooped up in one place.

Once Cody opened his eyes in the morning, his gas pedal was to the floor. Unlike some of the other misfit dogs I'd found whose full-blast energy meant a deluge of overwhelming action, Cody's energy was more a set of conniving, mental calculations. He was nothing short of an escape artist, and used his energy to constantly break out of any constraints put around him. He was impressive in his creativity, using his paws to knock open latches and go for a joyride. His first home returned him.

Cody's genial façade and handsome profile made anyone looking at him think he was nothing more than the sweetest dog in the world. Like a master thief who is able to burgle priceless art museums and then charm his way out from the police, Cody seemed above suspicion to any would-be adopter. House two was no match for his skills. Neither was house three. Somewhere in between, Cody found he could bump open lightly closed gates with a strong nudge from his nose or his rump.

A fourth house returned him.

A fifth house returned him.

Cody, of course, didn't mean to be recalcitrant. One of his greatest characteristics was a need to please, and he would try *so* hard. Anyone could see that, and so there were more willing to give him a chance.

Despite knowing well what they were getting into, a sixth house returned Cody. He was just eighteen months old when a seventh house brought him back.

When his downward tumble finally came to an end, Cody found himself in a Wisconsin Golden Retriever rescue. His record was finally too large for his charm to overcome. There were no more families willing to adopt him. The rescue was a no-kill shelter and he was likely to be a lifer, but that's not the way a free-spirited dog with a desire to please wants to live.

Cody caught one more break. The staff at the rescue had good heads on them and recognized that a good place for Cody—perhaps the only place—would be in the working dog world. They'd heard of the SDF after 9/11 and reached out to us.

At his evaluation, Cody swooped and slithered and strutted like the master escape artist he was. He displayed every ounce of prey drive, strength, and agility we needed for a search dog. Everyone at the foundation was excited when we took in Cody. It was stories like these that made us happy to be giving rescue dogs a second chance. Cody joined fellow tough-puppyhood survivor Ace at Sundowners to turn his mischievous talents into usable ones. I didn't expect any issues.

It was a few months into Cody's training when Pluis called me. I could hear the strain in her voice. She informed me we might have a problem with the slippery Golden.

"Is he not taking to obedience?" I asked.

"He's doing fine with obedience," Pluis replied.

"Is he having issues with the obstacles?"

"No. He's wonderful on the obstacles."

"Why are we not preparing to give him to a firefighter then?"

Pluis explained she'd noticed the issue every time she released Cody from a task and brought him back to her.

The last few steps he would slow, and then slink. Not a big deal, but it was what came next that troubled her greatly. Cody would not look her in the eye.

I knew that wasn't a good show of confidence for a dog but I was a little confused as to why Pluis was so concerned.

"He doesn't have trust," Pluis said with an air of finality.

Then it clicked. Trust between dog and handler was absolutely critical. If one party did not trust the other, there would be no way they could search effectively. They would not be a team. Trust was how all our teams made it through seemingly unconquerable rubble piles like Ground Zero. Pluis was correct; this wasn't a minor issue, it was an enormous, showstopping issue.

Nobody wanted to give up on Cody. Pluis concluded if she could slowly work him through the rest of the training, he might be able to regain trust. Only time would tell.

I agreed, hung up, and worried. I'd wondered if we'd ever run into a rescue whose psychological scars were insurmountable. It seemed like in Cody, we might've met our match. Trust and affection—indicated by looking the handler in the eyes—usually comes very naturally to Goldens. As Pluis likes to say, they love everybody! It was heartbreaking to imagine how torn up inside Cody must have been to shun that instinct. Seven different houses and a shelter in a turbulent eighteen months had left him with an inability to trust anyone who came into his life. How could he? Everything he'd done up to this point was *No! No! Bad dog!* Even if we were somehow able to explain to Cody that things would be stable now, he'd have no reason to believe us. There are certain things that just cannot be trained out of dogs, and Cody might very well have been broken beyond repair.

ELEVEN MONTHS IN, nearly double what our previous dogs took for training with Pluis, Cody still wasn't making eye contact. He was doing everything else well. He'd channeled all his energy into his work and he was excelling. Obedience and commands were no problem. Obstacles and agility were easy. His searching was top-notch. But when Pluis would give a command, Cody would look at her and then, seven homes and a shelter would come back. He'd look away, still refusing to trust.

I had to make the tough call. The SDF would always stand by our rescues, whether they became search dogs or house dogs, but obviously for Cody the latter was easier said than done. He'd never be abandoned again of course, but would that be the rest of his life? A constant quest for a home that could handle him? I didn't want to imagine what that would do to a dog already so traumatized he couldn't look a person in the eye. At the same time, I had the responsibility to rescue and train other candidates, many with similar backgrounds as Cody. Again, I faced the general's dilemma. I had to make the sacrifice for the greater good. I told Pluis we needed to move Cody along into a forever home.

Pluis overruled me. She said Cody needed just a little more time. I didn't want to be heartless, but I was hesitant. The more time Cody spent, the longer another candidate had to wait. But I'd built a strong and knowledgeable team whose input I valued. I, like Cody, had to trust her. I agreed. He would have one more shot.

IT WAS FALL of 2002, and the weather in Southern California was starting to chill. The green grass of the training field at Sundowners Kennel had browned in the late autumn, thirsty for the winter rains. Pluis, working by herself, stood on the field and watched Cody run through a series of training tasks without error. The young Golden was doing everything right. His clever way of problem-solving that had served him so well as an escape artist now allowed him to work through any obstacle. He would make a great search dog, if only he could learn to trust again. Pluis could feel the pressure. His time with her was nearly up. She'd tried everything in her bag of training tricks and he still wasn't looking her in the eye. It was something he needed to work out himself. She could only pray.

Cody, his dog smile beaming, nattily conquered the final obstacle and Pluis called his name. He looped back to where she was standing, his amber coat flowing like falling leaves across the autumn afternoon.

"Cody, heel," Pluis commanded.

Cody, unwanted and without a home or much of a future at all, obediently took up his proper position, close by her side. Then he leaned against her and looked up, directly into her eyes.

Pluis started to cry.

SHE CALLED ME and with a shriek of glee informed me of the good news. Cody was ready to be paired with a handler. He would need someone with a gentle touch who could maintain his fragile bridge of trust, but he was *ready*. I doubt if anyone besides Pluis could have successfully rehabilitated Cody. Now, instead of scrambling to set up an unstable dog in a precarious home life, we were adding another team to our roster.

CODY WAS PARTNERED with Chula Vista, California, firefighter Linda D'Orsi, a quiet but driven woman with both a gentle touch and an unrelenting toughness. Cody no longer had trust issues, and bonded with Linda immediately. He embraced his new home life, family, and the other Golden Retriever Linda had as a pet. The dog who'd never known a family now had a permanent family, the adoration of a fire department, and even a sibling. Cody seemed to recognize his good fortune. Gone were his escape artist days. When a non-search call came in for Linda and the other firefighters, Cody was happy to sit in the truck, seat belt fastened, patiently waiting until his partner returned. When it came time to search, Cody practically broke down the walls of his crate to get to work and please his new family.

During a search, Golden Retrievers usually hang their tails low. But Cody was too proud to. He held his tail high as he searched, like a Golden flag. Cody also developed an enigma of a bark alert. Goldens typically alert in short, almost-chirpy barks. Cody's bark was a low, guttural roar that echoed across the rubble pile and announced to the world that this is what he was made to do.

Thirty-two

NOT QUITE MAKING
THE CUT

Over the years at the SDF we've seen all types of dogs with all types of issues. Adopting a rescue is always a roll of the dice. We've seen many multiple-return dogs like Cody. We had one crazy stray listed as a "police impound." We've had multiple eleventh-hour euthanasia saves like Ace. We had dogs that would jump on top of the wooden fence at Pluis's kennel and use it as a balance beam, just to see what was happening on the other side. We adopted a dog so out of control, the only thing on his adoption sheet listed for behavior was one word: "Unsalvageable."

With Cody successfully paired, the SDF's success rate in producing search dogs was above 90 percent. But of course there were those dogs that didn't make the cut. We'd committed to never put our candidates back into shelters, but dogs like Cody presented an interesting co-nundrum: What do we do if the dog *needs* some type of a job, but for one reason or another, can't be a search dog? Many of our candidates had so much energy, it would be almost cruel to force them into a "normal" house life. The answer, we found, was put them to work! Just . . . a dif-ferent kind of work.

Zorro was a German Shepherd the color of coal, ex-cept for his gold nugget eyes. He had fantastic athletic abil-ity and good prey drive. He could dart and cut around rubble piles with a series of sharp fencing moves just like his masked hero eponym—*Left, right, left and ahha! I've got you!* But Zorro had an interesting weakness come out dur-ing training. He would often get distracted during searches. Not by people or loud equipment or other dogs, but by plants. He would sometimes pause mid-search to give the local fauna a good sniff. It was actually quite hu-morous. He was like the child who picks flowers while the other kids play soccer around him. The dog clearly had talent, but we couldn't rely on him for a life-and-death search. Fortunately, we found a perfect niche to combine his talent and his "hobby." After a period of retraining, Zorro began a new career as an ecological detection ca-nine, focusing on finding exotic plant species. Zorro now would comb the forest floor, bobbing and weaving through towering conifers, ahead of a scientist, and seek out endangered species of plants and animals for research. Among the scents he would imprint on were an endangered lizard species and an endemic shrew species. Zorro was a shoo-in and could now spend all the time he wanted smelling the roses.

Chewy was a petite Golden Retriever with a sanguine auburn coat who'd been surrendered twice because he was just too much to handle. Chewy's immense prey drive more than compensated for his small stature, and the dog was brought in to start training. But in fact, Chewy's prey drive was so intense that he would start competing against other dogs and exhibiting antisocial behavior. He wanted it to be a one-dog show. Because searchers work in teams and our dogs can't show any type of aggression or antisocial behavior, Chewy needed a career change. There was a calling that needed a solo star, and even treated him to a complimentary hotel room once his work was done. Chewy began his new career sniffing out bedbugs. He would travel to hotels and nursing homes, his keen nose and high prey drive beating out any human technology to root out the nasty little creatures. He might not have made a search dog, but we all slept better at night knowing Chewy was on call.

Axel was a mix of about thirty different breeds, but probably pointer was most prominent in his physical appearance—a chocolate and vanilla coat stretched across a sleek frame, pointed at both ends with a short tail and sharp nose. This interesting young pup was rescued from a shelter in northern Idaho near the Canadian border. Initially Axel passed our candidate screening, but when it came down to it, he couldn't hold together a full run through a search course. We knew Axel was more than capable, though, and thought he could move into some kind of detection work. After a brief period of retraining, Axel was partnered with a law enforcement handler where he served as a contraband detection dog in detention facilities—searching out illegal cell phones, drugs, and other banned items that inmates tried to smuggle in. His services became so sought after, Axel and his handler would travel all over the state to different facilities. The pointer learned to love life on the road and especially took to the hotel beds at night—some of them probably cleared of bedbugs by Chewy.

SOMETIMES WE HAD handlers that weren't quite up to snuff, either. Training can be a tough teacher, and Pluis did not allow mistakes to be ignored. At one training event, a dog was having a tough time with an obstacle and the handler started berating the dog. This is never ok. Ever. This type of treatment is especially detrimental when the dog is still mentally building trust with the handler and can have permanent consequences.

Pluis and I have something else in common: you don't want to get on our bad side, especially when it comes to the dogs. She got right in the handler's face like she was about to start a fistfight.

"If you fuck up my dog," she snarled, no more than an inch from the handler's face, "I will *fuck you up!*"

She stared the handler down for another minute, then turned her back to him and stomped away.

Jim Boggeri, working with Recon on the other side of the kennel, remembers watching the confrontation and being scared stiff, standing at attention as Pluis marched past, her face a hard mask of anger. He was afraid to breathe. But in classic Pluis fashion, when she saw Jim's petrified eyes, she dropped him a subtle wink.

Thirty-three

RECON AGAINST THE MACHINE

(or the Monday Night Football Incident)

E ven some of our qualified search dogs had a tough time staying on track with a search career. Search dogs are the punk rock of the service dog world—they have tons of energy and heart, but perhaps not the greatest respect for authority. Every once in a while they need to buck the system and run with the wild mustangs. As Ana, the SDF poster princess had demonstrated, even with her extensive training, sometimes a girl just wants to have fun (and pancakes).

As I've already recounted, Recon probably did this more often than the other dogs. His handler, Jim Boggeri, likened search dogs to frat boys and sorority girls: every day was a party. Recon took this description to heart and didn't mind making a public scene of it. Perhaps his most famous showcase occurred in front of a national audience on Monday Night Football.

On October 20, 2003, the SDF dogs were invited to do an agility demonstration for the halftime show at an Oakland Raiders game. It was a fantastic opportunity to display the prowess and skill of our dogs. We'd come a long way from intermission at local horse races.

As soon as the Raiders and Chiefs hit the locker rooms, the Oakland Coliseum staff was rolling out tunnels and balance beams and teeter-totters for a demonstration of the SDF's best-trained dogs. Ten dogs and their handlers were given the signal to go, and ran out of the corner end zone entrance to roaring applause. Over sixty-three thousand fans were on their feet cheering the firefighters. The ground shook with thrilled shouts and the heavy metronome of chants. Jim kept Recon on a close lead, but it was difficult not to be excited by the thunderous applause. Just as he would during any search, Jim tried to stay focused directly on the task at hand.

The event narration began and the dogs were put through the agility course. They all settled into the routine of the task and smoothly completed one obstacle after another. All of them, except for Recon.

As Recon finished the balance beam, he was supposed to perform a sit-stay command. Recon made it about halfway through the sit . . . then stopped and looked back over his shoulder at Jim. Jim knew the look and it made his blood freeze. It was Recon's *Watch this, Dad!* look. Jim started to scream *NOOOOO* but Recon was already gone. With only his devil-may-care doggy grin, Recon sprinted out of the confines of the agility course and down the field for a touchdown.

Jim screamed. The crowd roared.

Recon obeyed the crowd and started sprinting large victory laps around the entire field.

The crowd went crazy. Jim buried his face in his hands. When he looked up, there was his wild Lab, live on the JumboTron.[1]

Eventually, Recon made it back to his distraught handler. All Jim could do was laugh. You can take the wolf out of the wild, but not always the wild out of the wolf.

The next day, when Jim returned to his Marin County firehouse, his chief called him in. Jim prayed it was somehow a coincidence and had nothing to do with the little halftime mishap. He was not so lucky. His chief had Raiders season tickets. He had been at the game along with a good portion of the firehouse. They let Jim have it immediately.

"Caught your little show last night, Jim!"

---

1 Only later would Jim admit regretting not making up some fake hand-command like a looping circle above his head to make it seem like it was all part of the show. Anyone on the inside would of course know different, but at least a stadium full of people wouldn't know he was that guy. Too soon old, too late wise.

"Ten-thousand-dollar dog? There's money well spent, Boggeri!"

"Jim, you didn't tell me Recon is Oakland's new running back!"

Jim could only grin and bear it.

In the background, Recon napped peacefully, his primal instincts resting. For the time being.

Thirty-four

A NEW ERA

n early 2005, through almost a decade of evolution, the SDF had produced sixty-four dogs. Of those, twenty-seven held FEMA Advanced certification and could deploy nationally or internationally. The attacks on 9/11 had taught us a great deal, as had numerous smaller, local deployments. We needed to absorb those lessons and improve. Everyone, from the handlers-in-training to canine recruiters to Pluis and myself, was taking these lessons to heart and asking how we could progress.

The SDF was still mostly staffed by loyal volunteers, and I still managed day-to-day operations. I was approaching seventy-two years young. John had passed away, but I was starting to acquire grandchildren. There are only so many nights you can fall asleep working at your desk, the hour well beyond midnight, before it gets old. I wanted to stay part of the foundation, but for the day-to-day operations I wanted to keep our momentum fresh with someone who had been in the trenches more recently than I, someone as dedicated to my vision as I was. I knew just the person: my protégé, Debra Tosch.

For Debra, promotion to executive director was bittersweet. It would mean she would be hanging up her handler's leash and saying goodbye (temporarily) to Abby, who still had many good years of searching left in her. But Debra also knew that for the greater good, stepping up would serve best. So, the wheels were set in motion. Neither of us knew she'd have another encore as a handler before her time was up.

All around the foundation, things were changing. Ana, our phenomenal leading lady for so many years, was aging gracefully, a tinge of white-gray now sprinkled her face. She would be retiring soon. As would the other pilot program Goldens, Dusty and Harley. And Zack and Sherman and Manny and a number of the other dogs, now seasoned veterans. But you couldn't tell them that. The dogs had barely slowed. They loved their jobs and would've continued searching until their last breaths. The handlers knew better, though. The body can only take so much; they knew it wouldn't be long before they would be selecting comfy couches for their partners to relax in retirement.

In the meantime, the veteran teams stayed busy help-ing train the up-and-coming dogs and handlers. Our group of new recruits was learning and maturing fast. Ace was FEMA Advanced certified, as well as his seven-time homeless Golden Retriever comrade, Cody. Fire Captain Jim Boggeri and his aspiring NFL running back partner, Recon, were appointed as the SDF San Francisco Bay Area training group leaders, overseeing all canine training sessions in the region. Even party boys have to grow up sometimes.

Pluis had brought in her daughters, Kate and Sharon, to help train the ever-increasing number of dogs we were sending her. At the time, they had their hands full trying to get a talented-but-troublesome Border Collie named Hunter through training.

The winds of change were certainly blowing all over the organization.

ON AUGUST 23, 2005, some much stronger winds began to blow in the Caribbean Sea. Warm water swelled and fu-eled winds faster and faster as a tropical storm worked its way over the Bahamas and up over the southern tip of Florida. The winds spun like a top and revved up past Cat-egory 1 levels. By the time it made landfall in southern Mississippi six days later, Hurricane Katrina was generat-ing sustained winds of over 175 mph.

Thirty-five

NOTHING LEFT BUT SPLINTERS

As the winds from Katrina's epicenter finally died out some 150 miles inland from the gulf, the nation looked on at the aftermath of one of the most destructive natural disasters in US history. Large portions of Louisiana, Mississippi, and other areas along the Gulf Coast were in ruins. In small towns, houses had been reduced to matchsticks. New Orleans, battered first by the wind and rain from Katrina, then experienced a massive failure of its 350-mile levee system. In under eighteen hours, almost 80 percent of the city was flooded by anywhere between six to twenty feet of destructive water. The widespread devastation and thousands of displaced people quickly put a strain on federal and local emergency services, ill prepared for a disaster of this magnitude and now responsible for what would be the largest SAR operation in history.

The SDF dogs were ready. When the call came, twenty-six SDF-trained canine search teams spread across the twelve FEMA task forces responded. This was double the number of teams we'd sent to Ground Zero, but unlike the steel pile of the 9/11 aftermath, stacked high and deep, the leftovers from the hurricane were spread far and wide, over ninety-three thousand square miles, with a lot of it still under water. The search teams would once again have to adapt and learn on the fly for their new mission.

Their primary job would be searching voids where a human could survive. What made this task complicated was the expanse of the destruction—an estimated three hundred thousand homes destroyed across 138 counties. Entire cities had been deemed without an inhabitable structure. The amount of rubble left behind was estimated at 118 million cubic yards. To put this in perspective, if this amount of rubble was compressed into the footprint of Ground Zero, the rubble pile would reach 140 miles high. A search by humans would take years, but with the dogs they could search the perimeter of sites in a matter of minutes, committing rescue squads only if the dogs showed interest.

The overall organization of the rescue effort made things difficult. Unlike the 9/11 attacks, federal response to the hurricane was slower, and military aircraft were not available to transport the task forces. Our teams had to drive themselves across the Gulf Coast in convoys of vans and commercial buses. It took a number of days for the task forces to even get into Texas. Jim Boggeri, with Recon resting up for his first deployment in the back, remembers white-knuckling a van down the Texas interstate, trying to keep the wind from blowing them off the road. Once they got to Houston, they were again stymied as they were put on standby for proceeding farther until the civil unrest in the storm-affected cities was controlled. The hold lasted almost three days, and dramatically lowered the chance of the teams finding any trapped victims alive.

When our teams finally received the go-ahead, they spread out between Gulfport and Biloxi in Mississippi, and New Orleans in Louisiana. When they arrived, there was still a great deal of confusion. A number of local volunteers had taken it upon themselves to take their own "search dogs" out onto the rubble. I commend their willingness to help, but these dogs were not certified in any sense and the handlers were not professionally trained. In one instance, an untrained Poodle, dyed bright pink, had to be pulled off a rubble pile. The act was done with good intentions, but if you're not a pro, you're doing more harm than good.

For this deployment, there were a number of our rookie teams leading the charge. Cody went into New Orleans. Ace, the Yellow Lab who'd survived pepper spray and abandonment, and Recon, our free-spirited platinum Lab, went to Gulfport. There were also a good number of familiar faces. Ana and Dusty, our first two SDF dogs, aging but still on top of their game, came with firefighters Rick and Randy to Gulfport. Chocolate Lab prodigy Zack and crazy guy Duke also made up the team. Debra Tosch, called away from her new executive director position, brought our star Abby, and Abby's best bud in the world, Border Collie Manny, with handler Ron Weckbacher.

With all these veterans, the teams thought they had plenty of experience to go around. Searching Ground Zero after 9/11 had been a crucible, but most were confident in what was to come. What they found was not at all what they were prepared for.

ANA LEAPT OUT of the air-conditioned van and ran into a wall of 102-degree heat and humidity. Compared to the frigid nights in New York City, the late August heat of Mississippi's second-largest city was oppressive.

The heat would be a major limiting factor. The handlers would have to keep an eye on the dogs, who would go until they collapsed and then go some more. Besides the vans, there was practically no shelter from the heat. The teams would eventually start to bolus fluids to the dogs, essentially IVing them a preemptive camel's hump of hydration that would slowly absorb into the dog's system. There was no shade. Any trees left standing—which were few—had been denuded by the hurricane's fury.

There were practically no structures standing in Ana's search area. If viewed from space, the hurricane spins like a counterclockwise circular saw blade with the northeastern quadrant as the cutting edge—the strongest and often most dangerous place to be in a hurricane. Gulfport and Biloxi had been in the northeastern quadrant of the storm. The cities now looked like the hand of God had been dragged across the once-green landscape. Large semitrucks had been tossed like toys in the storm surge. Concrete stairs led up to nothing. A large casino built on a floating barge had been flipped upside down and smashed like a cake dropped from a countertop, with tiny pieces scattered like spilled sprinkles. All the residential structures were demolished and blended together in a river of debris. For blocks and blocks in each direction, the rescuers couldn't tell where one house stopped and another started. They could only estimate general "boxes" to search.

Of all the landscaping and building materials, there seemed to be only splinters left. For the veteran teams from 9/11, this was a whole new ball game. Again, the teams were facing a search puzzle they'd only scraped the surface of in training. But firefighters adapt.

Rick Lee looked down at Ana, who sat calmly by his

side, but was already panting in the heat. "Ready search?" he asked. Ana was on like a light switch, the heat forgotten.

One by one, and block by block, Ana and the rest of the teams started to clear their boxes.

DUSTY AND RANDY Gross didn't let the daunting miles of search area slow them either. In a lot of the residential areas, shattered wood was stacked high overhead. These piles were unstable, and usually couldn't support the weight of a human searcher. Moats of thick mud or water surrounded the structures. The wood made for difficulty in access, the broken struts and spars woven together, making plenty of voids to trap a victim, but not nearly large enough for a rescuer to squeeze through. A human rescuer, that is. Dusty moved freely over the piles, winding through mud and squeezing into voids too small for her partner. Her focus didn't wane.

Because the houses were essentially put through a washing machine, much of their contents were strewn across the rubble piles. It was not uncommon to find open refrigerators and pantries with food dumped everywhere. The food was contaminated at this point, but even rancid food can smell good to a hungry dog. The SDF handlers use a toy as a reward instead of a treat for this reason. Spoiled and exposed food is common in disaster areas and cannot be a distraction for the search. It also cannot be consumed due to its health risks for the dogs. The SDF dogs wanted the food, but they knew to stay away from it.

Dusty, however, faced probably the largest test of will when she happened on the ultimate temptation. She was searching an area where a large shipping container, the kind you see on the back of a semitruck, had flipped and the impact had blown out the doors. The trailer lay like a crushed burrito, its contents spilling out. Dusty rounded the trailer and found a mountain of frozen chickens. Thousands of them. Dusty no doubt thought she'd died and gone to heaven. But she knew food was off-limits so she cast a baleful glance back at Randy. Randy said no. With an *aww man* snort, Dusty went right back to searching, the forbidden fruit no longer in her mind. Randy felt a little sorry for her, but knew it was for everyone's good.

ZACK AND HIS handler, Jeff Place, along with Recon and Jim Boggeri, worked their way from the coast northward into Biloxi, Mississippi. The area had been almost completely leveled from the storm surge. Anyone unlucky enough to be trapped in a collapse during the hurricane's onslaught likely drowned shortly after. With how much time had passed before the rescuers arrived, the search had already officially been deemed a recovery operation. But they pressed on with their mission. Zack and Recon were both hard-charging Labs and could cover a lot of ground quickly. If they indicated live scent anywhere, another dog from the task force could be brought in to fine-tune the search. For now, the searchers wanted to clear as much ground as possible, as quickly as possible.

Zack wriggled through small crawl spaces, into attics with the roofs opened like tin cans, and through windows whose blinds hung tattered and pointed in different directions. The dogs had been trained to find unconscious victims as well, even if they were freely exposed—it would do no good if they ignored an injured, unconscious person just because they weren't trapped in rubble. But in this case, Zack only found the dead. Much like Ground Zero, the dogs were searching for a miracle, a live find. But they would also help bring closure by finding deceased victims. Zack and Jeff would mark the bodies for extraction, or call in a cadaver-specific dog if Zack was indicating but couldn't pinpoint the source.

The teams found a rooftop, perfectly intact, settled on top of what looked like a stack of scrap lumber. It was as if the hurricane had lifted up the roof, demolished the house beneath, then set the roof gingerly back down again. It had been a couple-story house, so there were certainly void spaces underneath, but no direct route inside. Jim and Jeff cut a hole into the roof. The sawdust from the chainsaw had barely settled before Recon was perched on the hole, ready to search. Recon's call-of-the-wild days were not necessarily behind him (probably never would be), but he seemed to understand the gravity of his first major deployment. He was the model of focus and discipline. In he went, and Jim followed.

The bright afternoon sun was immediately cut off and the team was engulfed in darkness. The void beneath the roof was so shallow Jim had to belly-crawl. As he did, he noticed a hard, familiar surface beneath him. His flashlight revealed pocked and gray asphalt. He was on what used to be the street. As he surveyed the rest of his surroundings, he was struck by another odd site. Most of the house's living room furniture was still upright and intact, arranged as it might've been when the house was standing. The complete living room set now rested in eerie composure on the street underneath the misplaced roof, as if it had gone out for the afternoon, and then forgotten where it left the rest of the house. The stench of mold and rotten fish was overwhelming. The heat inside cooked like an oven. It was a horrible environment to search. But like he often did, Jim remembered Tim McSweeney and the rest of the FDNY Ladder companies. They'd done their jobs without question. Jim and his four-legged partner would do the same. They carried on.

The numerous alcoves under the roof still had too much debris for Jim to move freely, but Recon was more than happy to search anywhere. Jim would send him down a void, one dark tunnel at a time, and listen to his scampering paws until he reached a stopping point. Then they'd do it again. Each time Recon would come back happy and ready to go once more. They kept going because, just like the firefighters in Ladder Company 3, there were others counting on them.

Later, after Recon had finished searching, Jim passed one of these others, an elderly man standing by a debris pile of what used to be his house. The man was tall and thin. His eyes were vacant. The team stopped to talk to the man and check if he needed any supplies. Jim struck up a conversation. The man told his tale. He said he'd awoke, just one day after retiring from his lifelong job, to see water pouring into the intersection at the top of his street. He'd had enough time to wake up his wife and move her upstairs. Water battered down their door and flooded the first floor. They fled to the second floor. The water rose to the second floor. The man lifted his wife into the attic, but couldn't make it up there himself. The water continued to rise. When the water reached the bottom of the attic, the man thought he was going to drown. Then the water receded, leaving the man alive but the house destroyed and the family's possessions gone. "I lost everything," the man said and started crying.

The rescuers would hear similar stories from all they talked to. The crew would check on people throughout the day, have the dogs search, then let the dogs rest. Then they would push forward, another box, another block, another mile of indistinguishable splinters.

In the evening, as the sun sunk to a blood red horizon, one local couple who'd lost everything except a small refrigerator cart walked around the FEMA BOO, selflessly handing out ice cream to firefighters.

NOT FAR WEST, New Orleans hadn't been spared much of the brunt of the storm. But whereas Mississippi took the high winds, New Orleans's biggest issue was flooding after the levee system surrounding the city failed. Only hours after Katrina hit, the storm surge was pounding the Gulf Coast, Lake Borgne from the east, and curling north through Lake Pontchartrain. The city was under siege from all sides. The buffering wetlands were filled. Intracoastal waterways and other barriers were topped. All pumping stations and drainage areas were overwhelmed. The water could do nothing but rise. By the next day, many areas of the city had standing water deep enough to swallow a basketball hoop, backboard and all.

Cody, the lanky Golden who'd seen the inside of so many homes, now saw houses in a whole new way. Many had been flooded up to the eaves, their furniture tossed around inside and out like they'd come through a dishwasher. Water still covered much of the city. As Cody and Linda D'Orsi made their way across the flooded city with multiple other search teams from California and Florida, there was only so much the dogs could search. The water that still blanketed much of the city wasn't fresh water, or even normal seawater. Much like the contaminated food, the water after a Hurricane presents a major and often overlooked danger to rescuers, human and canine alike. Floodwater becomes a soup with everything that was once aboveground now added as hazardous ingredients—trash, fertilizer, human waste, dead humans and animals. There had been multiple oil and gas leaks encompassed in the estimated ninety-six million dollars' worth of damage, and all the harmful chemicals that come with such spills were deposited into the water. Coupled with the hot oven temperatures and soggy humidity, the water was nearly toxic. Any exposure would warrant immediate decontamination procedure. The dogs could swim—and some didn't mind—but they'd been trained to avoid the water for this exact reason. Many searches had to be done visually by the firefighters as the dogs waited. In houses where the water was low enough the dogs could search, getting in wasn't much easier. Thick mud covered everything. It was so deep in areas, it would suck up the firefighters' work boots, all the way past their white plastic kneepads. The dogs didn't let conditions get them down. When it was their time to search, they would bound, slip, claw, and kick their way into a void and back out again. House by house. Block by block.

Cody was assigned to search a building in Xavier University in Gert Town, New Orleans. He led the way, floor by floor, clearing offices and classrooms. There was evidence people had been stranded there, but eventually left once the waters receded. In one room, Cody found another dog who'd taken shelter from the storm. No one knew if the dog had an owner or if the owner had survived.

For a group of handlers now piloting rescue dogs it was a difficult sight. What made it more difficult was they could not take the dog with them. There were hundreds if not thousands of stranded pets in the area that needed care. The rescuers needed to focus on finding trapped people in need. Another unit would come by later to rescue the animals, but it made it no less difficult for the firefighters. Linda left the dog food and plenty of fresh water. With a heavy heart, she turned and led Cody out of the university for another search. She could only hope the stray got another shot at a new life, just like Cody had years ago.

Not long after this search, all canines were pulled from the search effort as recovery operations shifted into high gear. The dogs were no longer needed, but the firefighters could still help out. They would finish out the deployment helping clear rubble, treating injuries and other medical conditions, and lending a hand wherever someone needed it. By mid-September, the teams were back home to prepare for the next deployment.

DEBRA TOSCH HAD barely cleaned the Mississippi mud off Abby's paws when the call to respond to Hurricane Rita came in. A category 5 hurricane, Rita tore up eastern Texas and western Louisiana less than a month after the devastation of Katrina. We deployed eighteen SDF teams to Rita, many the same as the teams who'd responded to Katrina. They were spread from Dallas to Houston and down into New Orleans and the Louisiana coast where the storm surge had again topped the already-breached levees. One notable addition was Harley, our kind soul and pilot program dog. With Ana and Dusty already deployed to Hurricane Katrina, Harley was the last of the original three to gain a hurricane deployment under his collar before retirement.

Harley and Rob Cima made their way to Houston with San Diego Task Force 8. The winds were still over 100 mph as they waited in their hotel to search.

Rob took Harley outside to relieve himself. They exited on the leeward side of the hotel in a distinct wind shadow. Not thinking much of it, Rob sent Harley out to a patch of grass beyond the hotel. As soon as Harley cleared the hotel's wind shadow the hurricane winds snatched him and lifted him off his feet. Harley then began somersaulting across the open field like a tumbleweed. He finally regained his footing and hightailed it back to a shocked Rob, now with a new appreciation of how strong the winds were. Welcome to Rita.

FROM THERE, THE rescue effort for Hurricane Rita was much less eventful. On the ground, Abby and Debra found a carbon copy of the Katrina deployment. Miles and miles of houses and structures turned into scrap wood. Sweltering temperatures and drowning humidity. Many of the same areas had to be searched again. Fortunately, many of the already-devastated areas were abandoned and could not be further damaged. Residents had used the earlier hurricane as a siren song and evacuated prior to Rita's arrival. Where fatalities from Katrina were in the thousands, fatalities from Rita were under two hundred.

The searchers might've wanted some time off between deployments, but the dogs were more than ready to search again. Abby covered each pile with the precision she was known for, checking every nook and void until the heat wore her out. She would rest a spell, then do it again. The search period was much shorter than Katrina and very quickly became a recovery effort. The dogs were sidelined for some much-needed rest while the firefighters continued to help with other tasks in the disaster cleanup.

BY LATE SEPTEMBER 2005, all eighteen teams had returned home safe and another SDF chapter was closed. We'd learned many new lessons and gained valuable experience from the hurricanes. I couldn't have been more proud of our foundation.

For the pilot program, and most of the 9/11-era search dogs, the hurricanes in the gulf would be their last major deployment. Ana, Dusty, and Harley, the three dogs who had set the standard and made everything possible, would retire over the next few years. Ana would continue to climb the ladder to the top of the house to help Rick put up Christmas lights every holiday. With Harley in retirement, Rob Cima inherited Ace, who'd grown from the abandoned and abused pup into a world-class searcher. After Katrina, Ace's deployment schedule slowed down. Wanting to keep the dog engaged and utilize some of his advanced training, Rob got him certified as a hospital therapy dog. Every week, a jolly Ace would accompany Rob to Shriners Hospitals for Children in Sacramento and spread some of his infinite joy to the patients. The children loved him. It was a perfect job for a dog who could not be touched and hugged and loved enough.

Sherman, Manny, and Zack would follow the others into retirement not long afterward. In 2007, my heroic Black Lab, Murphy, my SDF founding partner and the best search dog I ever knew, passed away. She'd led an amazing life and helped set in motion what became the SDF. I saw her legacy in every dog we saved and trained. And it was in her undying spirit that we continued forward and turned the page again. She would've never wanted the search to stop.

Thirty-six

THE SEARCH MUST GO ON

Over the next few years, the SDF teams deployed to support searches for a number of close-to-home disasters. Mudslides in California are always a danger after rain. Recon and Jim Boggeri responded to a large mudslide in Mill Valley, California, where the slide had brought a large tree through a bedroom wall and down on top of the homeowner. Abby and Debra Tosch, along with nine other SDF teams, were called to a similar event in La Conchita, California. Cody, the seven-time homeless Golden, also responded to a mudslide in La Soledad, California, with handler Linda D'Orsi. All the teams performed very well on each deployment, but no live victims were recovered. The circumstances of the disasters didn't allow for a high probability of survivability for a buried victim, but the handlers couldn't help but wish they'd been able to find people alive.

IN EARLY 2007, LA County USAR Task Force canine coordinator, firefighter, and SDF handler Billy Monahan was meeting with international search teams to try to better prepare US-based disaster response. International disaster search dog teams usually came from Germany or Switzerland. These countries' teams deployed as small groups and often made it to disaster sites much faster than their US counterparts, who deployed as part of a fully equipped task force.

A tall man with a wide mustache that curled around his round face, Billy was a career firefighter and wanted to see dog teams on-site faster in order to save more lives. Saving a life wasn't a matter of skill. It was a matter of opportunity. At Oklahoma City and Ground Zero, the force of collapse was just too much to survive. Everything that wasn't steel was crushed into a powder. Any structure collapse, or landslide would be similar, and a factor we could never change. We had to accept that every time we'd be searching for one in a million. But Billy, as well as everyone in the SDF, knew as long as the chance for life existed, we wouldn't want the rescue response to be delayed a single second longer than necessary.

Wearing multiple hats at the time, Billy was also in the

middle of training his own SDF dog with a focus on scent dispersed over wide areas and multiple floors underground. His dog was a special dog. A dog so talented, he found victims before certification tests even started. A dog who, in the next few years, would play a historic role in the SDF.

THE DRIVE TO improve FEMA response times continued across the next three years until the afternoon of January 12, 2010, when a point on the Enriquillo-Plantain Garden fault beneath the Caribbean nation of Haiti ruptured, unleashing a magnitude 7.0 earthquake on the country. Many buildings in Haiti's capital, Port-au-Prince, were leveled. The numerous collapses meant an enormous death toll. For any people trapped alive after the earth stopped shaking, the clock was ticking.

Thirty-seven

BURIED ALIVE: HAITI

The women sat in the dark and waited to die.

Almost three days earlier, as the heavy afternoon heat crept over Port-au-Prince, the massive earthquake had stolen the ground from beneath their feet.

In terms of percentage of a country's population killed, the earthquake was the most destructive natural disaster ever in modern history. The earth shook so violently, the artificial ground fill making up the foundation for much of the port took on the properties of a liquid. For almost fourteen seconds, the firm ground became a quicksand-like trap, swallowing foundations and mercilessly toppling buildings. It turned an apartment where three young Haitian women resided into a prison of rubble.

The prison would soon be a tomb.

Three days without food or water slowed the women's shallow breaths with fatigue. There would be no escape under their own power. Like fighting a slowly constricting python, any struggle to push out would further collapse their cell. There would be no rescue from outside either. The curtains of mangled concrete withheld any indication to passersby the collapsed apartment had spared anyone from the terrible fate that had claimed almost 230,000 lives.

At the time of the quake, Haiti was the poorest country in the western hemisphere, with half its population living on less than US $1 a day. Disregard for building codes and regulations was commonplace. The resulting shortcuts left the majority of structures in the country well outside of what would be considered earthquake-safe construction. The consequences were dire: thirteen of fifteen key governmental buildings were in ruin, including the presidential palace and Parliament. Almost 90 percent of Port-au-Prince's sister city, Leogane, had been leveled.

International aid was beginning to trickle in, but the women's apartment was just another rubble pile in an entire city of rubble. Lacking the ability to signal to the outside world that they were alive, it was unlikely they would be saved by the already overwhelmed relief effort.

The women didn't need help. They needed a miracle.

Thirty-eight

HOLLYWOOD HUNTER

anding lights pierced the night sky as the helicopter came in low over the palm trees. It was coming for one dog.

The craft from the Kern County emergency services in Southern California hovered for a moment, then set down next to Fire Captain Billy Monahan. Billy, who'd served almost forty years in the fire service, knelt in an empty lot across from his house with the dog of the hour tight by his side as the rotor wash flattened the grass around them. It was a fitting entrance for a Border Collie who in his seven years had earned a reputation as having a flair for drama. He boasted a flowing lion's mane of copper fur, a snowy white underside, and a dollop of white just before the tip of his nose. This was Hunter.

Hunter wasn't a large dog, but he seemed to project the regal grandeur of royalty, giving an air of importance that people couldn't help but respect and admire. Hunter loved attention. His chest would puff proudly. His mouth would crack into the bright canine smile of a movie star. By design or fortune (but probably his own design), Hunter always managed to put his best paw forward when the cameras came around.

Hunter had been featured on numerous media programs. Anchors would swoon over the dog who always seemed to strike the right pose at the right time. A veteran of multiple deployments, Hunter had even appeared on a "Hurricane Katrina First Responders" charity edition of *Family Feud*, barking at host Richard Karn to triple the points during faceoff rounds.

Billy scooped up Hunter and loaded him in the back of the helicopter along with a few heavy bags of deployment equipment as the aircraft's rotors continued to scream. They needed to lift off as soon as possible. The call to deploy for Haiti had come shortly after the last aftershock, and Hunter and Billy, as part of USA Task Force 2, were slated to deploy. The other international deployment team from Fairfax, Virginia, was already out the door. Details were still sketchy, but Washington had decided the destruction was enough to warrant two FEMA task forces. Now, Hunter and Billy were about to fast-track to the FEMA staging area at March Air Reserve

Base some 140 miles south near Riverside, California. Billy held Hunter tight as the helicopter lifted off.

As the lights from his hometown fell away into the night, and dog and handler were again shrouded in darkness, Billy was reminded of a time when the lights had not shined so brightly on his Hollywood hound. Long before the FEMA certifications and prime-time news coverage, Hunter's first canine career had been an utter failure.

LIKE ANA, HUNTER was slated as a disability-assistance dog. A dog's discipline and control are absolutely critical for success in this field of service. Hunter had neither. The pup couldn't keep a lid on his boundless energy, constantly bouncing off the walls and overwhelming his paraplegic owner. Less than a year old, Hunter was rejected from the program.

Hunter was donated to the SDF soon after, where we welcomed his raw energy. But his problems didn't stop there. Not long after he graduated from Pluis's kennel with off the chart marks in most areas—especially cognitive ability—and paired with Billy, Hunter fell victim to a common Border Collie affliction: he was bored of the search game.

As an experienced handler, Billy had hit the ground running with Hunter, constantly training. In this case, though, the method backfired. Hunter would study the search patterns. He would study the judges at tests. He would study Billy. In true Border Collie fashion, he would commit them all to memory, analyze, and figure out a more efficient way to take care of his herd. It didn't take Hunter long to realize he could make the game much shorter and simpler by not giving a bark alert. He could find the buried victim, but why go through all that effort to bark when the handler would be along shortly? And why tug on the toy reward when he would much rather it just be left to him to do with as he pleased? To Hunter, that was just wasted energy.

We'd seen it before with herding dogs, especially Border Collies, but we'd usually been able to train them out of it. Hunter was a particularly difficult case. The whole SDF team was pitching in and drawing blanks. Billy spent hours on the pile trying different techniques with Hunter to no avail. No bark alerts, and no tug-of-war with the toy reward. It was like Hunter had forgotten his prey drive when he was on the pile. Billy began questioning everything. He felt like throwing up his hands in defeat—a slippery slope for a handler. If there are doubts in the handler, the dog can read them, and then the trust disappears and the team becomes all but useless during a real search.

One day, after another frustrating and fruitless training session, Billy was having a conversation with a teammate in the parking lot of his fire department. Hunter was behind him, being his usual neurotic self. The tug toy fell out of Billy's pocket and landed behind his boot. Without thinking much, Billy gave it a kick . . . and Hunter chased after it. Billy continued talking. Hunter brought the toy back and dropped it in the exact spot by Billy's boot. Billy kicked it again and sent it flying. Hunter pursued. He brought it back exactly like the first time, except he was even more energized and excited for another pursuit. Billy stopped talking, his attention now on Hunter.

Billy picked up the toy this time and tossed it. Hunter chased it down, snatched it off the asphalt, and shook it wildly while dancing a little victory jig. That was it. The final piece fell into place with a simple game of fetch. Billy figured out Hunter liked to pursue his quarry on his own terms. He also realized, unlike a ho-hum tug-of-war reward, Hunter never grew bored of *this* game because it brought a new excitement to the routine.

In his next mock search, Billy had the hidden victims drop or toss the reward toy when they were found instead of playing tug-of-war like normal. It worked like a charm. From then on, Hunter and Billy were unstoppable. During Hunter's FEMA certification exams, as Billy would walk Hunter up to the starting area, Hunter would suddenly jerk toward the pile. Billy knew Hunter had already found a victim. The actual test was a breeze.

Billy had evaluated search dogs all over the world; he would argue Hunter became one of the very best he'd ever seen. The pair would rack up over five hundred thousand frequent flyer miles traveling, training, and deploying together.

———

ON JANUARY 15, 2010, crammed in the back of a commandeered Chevy Blazer screaming across the fractured roads of Port-au-Prince, Hunter and Billy weren't exactly traveling first class. Twenty-four hours after touching down in Haiti, Billy knew this was a different ball game. He and his loyal partner were about to face the biggest challenge of their long career.

The destruction in the Caribbean nation was beyond comprehension. Still today Billy recalls the enormous number of dead; the bodies that hung from windows and fractured hallways; the stacks of bodies lining the streets; the overwhelming and inescapable stench.

Billy tried to stay positive because he knew his emotion transmitted up the leash to Hunter. He maintained the first responder's subconscious hope for survivors, no matter how dire the situation looked on the surface. But they were nearing the seventy-two-hour cusp since the disaster—the upper limit of the estimated time frame a trapped human can survive without food, water, and proper medical attention. Their first search of the presidential palace had turned up nothing but dead. Simple odds were they'd only find more bodies to add to the pile.

As the Blazer swung to a stop and opened its doors, Billy shook off the gnawing mental exhaustion and waded out into the thick humidity of the midday air, Hunter by his side. Time to focus—Hunter was up first, and the search did not look easy. What used to be an apartment was now a small mountain of rebar, trash, and jagged concrete chunks that stuck up like tombstones. The daunting size of the pile did little to raise spirits. Finding anything here would be difficult and dangerous.

Billy walked Hunter into position at the edge of the rubble and gave the small mountain another glance. No signs of life, but no time for doubt. There were an infinite number of sites to search, and that was barely scratching the surface. He looked down at his loyal partner. Hunter was sampling the air with his extraordinary nose and pulling the leash taut. No Hollywood drama here. The dog was ready to work.

Not knowing three lives were depending on what his dog did in the next five minutes, Billy unleashed Hunter and the search began.

HUNTER SPRANG FORWARD into air thick with scents of all types. A building collapse might dredge up buried odors or release trapped ones from within the walls, the building materials, or the surrounding ground, in addition to the scents that were already freely floating. Hunter was literally walking into a flood of smells.

Except he wasn't walking. He was bounding, bouncing from stone to stone like his feet were rubber. He bypassed a coil of razor wire, two metal chairs, and a broken window frame. Billy noticed his partner was picking up

speed as he neared a jagged arrangement of broken concrete. The concrete dropped into a crescent-shaped bowl
of rubble.

Billy tried to imagine the acrylic bubbles they would
use in training to show air currents, floating across the
remains of the structure. The air was hot here. Invisible
thermals rose from different locations and would fling
molecules off hard surfaces and send them ricocheting off
in different directions, an ever stirring pot of invisible
stew. Or maybe not moving at all—sometimes scent gets
trapped in buildings, especially thick concrete, and very
little escapes. A little extra pep in Hunter's step was nothing to get excited about yet, but did warrant some extra
attention.

Hunter crested the berm and descended into the small
depression. There were tiny crawl spaces, no more than a
foot and a half, into which Hunter would scrunch himself. He would penetrate the rubble pile so far back that
Billy could only see the bronze-circled reflection of his
eyes before he popped back out again. Hunter was focused.
All his training was coming through in his every movement.

Then it happened quickly. Hunter, who'd been
running an even straight line suddenly cut left like some
invisible wire had snagged him. The official term for this
is "hooked" and it literally looks like some offstage hook
in a cartoon reaches out and pulls the dog in a different

direction. Billy now had reason to get excited. Hunter was onto something.

Four stories below the surface, the three women still had no reason to hope. Any sounds of the search were unlikely to reach them. But their bodies were emitting dead cells from their skin, bacteria and organic matter in their breath, sweat from their pores, all of which could act like molecular rescue beacons for the sniffing machine circling above. As the molecules seeped out from the concrete, they hit more concrete; they mixed with the rest of the other scents—dirt and dust, rust and metal, bone and blood of the dead—diluting them, thinning them, masking them.

Somehow—maybe a lucky ricochet, maybe a favorable breeze—some of those molecules made it into Hunter's nose. The scent bounced through Hunter's nostrils, into one of his three hundred million or more sensory receptor sites and lit up his brain to human scent. *Live* human scent.

Hunter's search area grew smaller, more focused by the second. His body seemed to tighten. His tail began to wag.

Billy felt his pulse uptick slightly, but he tried to remain detached until he was sure. In his twenty-eight years involved with USAR, they had never been able to pull anyone out alive.

Then Hunter's search area was only a few square feet, focusing on nothing more than a tiny gap in the concrete.

He had something. Billy was certain of that now. But was it alive?

Then Hunter stopped. Whatever he was interested in, he'd found the apex of the scent.

Then he began to bark.

Billy waited no more. He called the find. He motioned to the interpreter, an elderly local man with hair the color of ash wearing a pink striped shirt and blue jeans, to call to the victim. Breathing hard, the man stumbled partway down the rubble toward Hunter, who was still barking at the crack. The man steadied himself. "Hail out!" he yelled in a thick French accent. He wanted to hear if the person trapped inside was alive. "Hail!" he called again.

Billy, still atop the crest and keeping an eye on Hunter, did not hear a response. If no one was alive, they would have to move on. There was too much destruction to waste time on more dead. But when the interpreter turned to face him, Billy knew they weren't going anywhere.

"They answered," the interpreter said, as if he were trying out the words for the first time.

Billy felt goose bumps prickle up his arms. There was no way anyone had survived this long. The countless dead were testament to that. Anyone could see that Port-au-Prince was a town of ghosts.

But then he was moving. His firefighter instincts propelling him down the steep face of the rubble, sliding and stumbling his way toward Hunter. He began hearing the muted voices coming from the gap in the concrete.

With a numb hand that felt detached from his body, Billy fumbled a water bottle out of his pack and secured it to the end of a stick with his glove. Tentatively, almost afraid the sounds of humans were merely apparitions and might disappear if approached too quickly, he stretched the stick forward into the crevasse. For a moment, only the unsupported weight of the water bottle hung heavy on the stick. Then something happened that Billy would later recall as the undisputed highlight of his forty-plus years of firefighting. Like hooking a fish after eighty-four days at sea, Billy felt a sharp tug and the weight of the water bottle was gone. Someone had grabbed it off the end of the stick. These people were alive.

Hunter sat expectantly, waiting for his reward,[2] and as Billy keyed his radio to bring the extraction crew, he heard something he'll never forget. From the depths of the rubble that had seemed to mock them at all the other sites, from where no one was supposed to survive, came a faint but clear voice:

"Thank you!"

IT TOOK TWO rescue squads—sixteen individuals—and a contingent of doctors almost seven hours to burrow down

---

2 Because of the excitement, Billy forgot to reward Hunter. He realized his mistake about an hour later and Hunter got his overdue game of fetch.

the four stories and free the young women. All three women were tired and injured, but alive. By the time they were being checked out by the medical staff, Hunter and Billy were already on to their next search.

BACK HOME, THE news traveled fast. I held out on any announcement until we were sure. Finally, with confirmation from multiple sources, word came: survivors found.

In our office in Ojai, I quietly gathered the small staff and volunteers of the foundation around and told them *they* were to credit for the victory. It was every ounce of energy that our team had poured into the SDF that led us here. The struggle of starting the foundation; the ups and downs of the pilot program; all the Americans who'd helped with donations, large and small; the deployments, major and minor—sixty-nine in total in 2010—that shaped our teams and training; Pluis and our trainers and all the firefighters and first responders who'd taken a chance with the foundation. Every one of these people was beside Billy as he pressed the water bottle into that void.

And although it was Hunter who'd found the victims, every SDF dog—135 trained search dogs at this point—was barking along with him.

Up at Sundowners Kennels, Pluis embraced her daughters. They sat with their dogs in a small courtyard between training areas, basking in the peaceful California breeze. They would laugh, then cry, then embrace and laugh again. They did this all day long.

In Sacramento, the Three Rs (Ana, Dusty, and Harley all having passed away, but with them in spirit) received the news like a welcome gift. These firefighters had forged the standards for handlers in the foundation and set the bar very high. They'd pioneered search techniques both for handlers and dogs. They'd helped mentor rookie handlers, including Billy with Hunter. Every veteran handler had contributed to enhancing training to some degree. In the moment of truth, this training had served.

I thought back over the last fifteen years. I thought about Oklahoma City, scouring the rubble with Murphy, and how I'd wanted nothing more than to pull someone out alive. Now we had. But mine wasn't the kind of celebratory moment that you'd expect. Above all, I had set out to start a great foundation for dogs that would save lives, so I saw this milestone as a waypoint along the path of a continuing journey. I acknowledged the importance of the events in Haiti, but didn't break my arm patting myself on the back. Now we needed to do it again, even if it took another fifteen years. It was the time to get back to work.

I DIDN'T HAVE to wait long. The other teams on the task force began finding people. A few days after their first find—the days were blurring together now for Hunter and Billy—Hunter was on another search in another collapsed multistory building outside of Port-au-Prince. The site was hundreds of square yards of broken and stacked concrete, but Hunter kept returning to a single crack in the wall. He didn't alert bark, but he would pace away then walk back to it and whine and whimper. Billy trusted his dog and called it.

They brought in a team with a hypersensitive listening device to try and further narrow down the search area. Their results were also inconclusive. They thought they might have heard a "fingernail scratching."

The team now faced a treacherous decision. Billy and the rescue squad had already been up digging through rubble for nineteen hours straight to rescue two young twins trapped in a building complex nearby. Saving the twins was pure elation, but just the day before that, the team was forced to abandon a search for another buried child. The child had been buried so deep, the rescue team couldn't narrow down an exact location in the rubble. During the hours of digging, the child had stopped responding to rescuers and the dogs no longer indicated a live scent. As devastating as it was, with thousands of potential victims and only a handful of rescuers, the decision to end the search was made.

Now, less than forty-eight hours later, Hunter was showing interest in what might be a similar situation. If there was a chance, however low, that someone could be rescued they decided they would trust Hunter's nose. As they'd done so often, the quiet professionals of the rescue squad began their backbreaking labor of digging for a miracle.

Seventeen hours later, through four floors of ten-inch concrete, the rescue teams broke through into a void. Rescuers crawled into the space and found a woman pinned against her mattress by the collapsed roof. The rescuers cut her out of the bed and pulled her to safety. She was alive and unharmed.

The weary rescue team, thirty-six hours on the job, walked the woman off the rubble. The sun was rising over the city with a restoring glow. A large crowd had gathered in the streets surrounding the rescue site. From the cracked roadways that had seen only destruction for days, the residents now looked on with hope. As the navy blue silhouettes of the rescue teams made their way to the surface, the jubilation of the crowd boiled over. The air that had only known a deathly silence for nearly a week now came alive, and a chant of *U-S-A! U-S-A!* echoed across the city.

THE FEMA TASK forces would return to the States on January 28, 2010. They were happy but exhausted in every way. They had poured themselves into every search. Besides Hunter and Billy, the other canine teams—Ron Weckbacher and Dawson, Ron Horetski and Pearl, Jason

Vasquez and Maverick, Gary Durian and Baxter, Jasmine Segura and Cadillac—all had played either a direct or supporting role in finding live victims in Haiti during separate searches. The support and rescue squads, who risked their lives through aftershocks and slugged through some of the hardest work on the planet digging through rubble, also cannot be overstated. Every rescue had been a true team effort. They did not care who was credited with what because what really mattered was that, in total, they had saved twelve lives from certain death.

BACK AT HIS home, where almost three weeks earlier a helicopter had landed to spirit him and his once-failed assistance dog away, Billy Monahan reflected on the experience. The catharsis of saving multiple lives and the unflinching determination of Hunter and the rest of the team, coupled with the outpouring of so much gratitude from a country that had so little, crashed over Billy in a deluge. He sat alone on his bed, letting the triumphs and heartbreaks flood him. It was too much. Billy felt the warm streaks of tears make their way down his cheeks. He let them flow freely. Then he felt the warm nuzzle of a familiar figure by his side. Buried as he was in emotion, Billy should not have been surprised to see his loyal partner.

Hunter, as always, had found him.

Wilma's Vision

AN AIRCRAFT BUZZES somewhere overhead as Wilma Melville takes in her empty hangar. The prop-driven airplane that once occupied the blank slab of concrete in front of us—a single-engine RV-7 sporting the original Black Lab logo of the SDF—is gone. A few days earlier, with her son as copilot, Wilma piloted the RV-7 cross-country to Maryland. The airplane stayed behind with her son, its move to the East Coast a one-way trip. Wilma returned to California flying commercial, a passenger this time.

"In aviation," she says, speaking of longevity in the profession, "you can go out like this," she eases one hand through the air in a smooth, diagonal descent, "or you can go out like this," she slaps her hands together.

Approaching eighty-five years old, Wilma has chosen

the former. With her airplane gone, the Santa Paula Airport hangar is now solely her living quarters. Two Dachshund-mixes, Newton and Darwin, Wilma's only roommates, lounge their sausage-like bodies on beds nearby, occasionally emitting a disconsolate whine to remind us of their impending dinnertime. The hangar has a small kitchen, bedroom, and built-in shower and is kept immaculately clean. Colored rugs and couch cover one side of the concrete, and portraits hang on the sheet metal walls. Despite its original purpose housing large flying machines, it still exudes the warmth of a home. But Wilma does not let herself get too comfortable. Stacked in the corner like a defiant counterpoint to any of the suburban luxuries is a stack of medicine balls, weights, and workout bands—Wilma's home gym. At least five days a week, she goes through a strength and conditioning routine, sometimes with a personal trainer, sometimes solo on her home rowing machine. At an age when most people would be lost without some type of assistance, it's quite clear Wilma could have many more years of piloting if she so chose.

But, as usual, Wilma sets a plan in her mind and executes it without looking back. Decades of relying on her own instincts, even against the odds, has long ago extinguished any thoughts of second-guessing herself. The results speak for themselves: Since the events described in 2010, the Search Dog Foundation has continued to grow at an exponential rate, raising over twenty-seven million dollars in private donations. The foundation's newly minted National Training Center is a sprawling facility covering 125 acres of donated ranchland in the foothills above Santa Paula. There are staged "disasters" and rubble piles for training, and housing for the dog handlers. A state-of-the-art kennel facility comes complete with doggy treadmills and grooming stations on pneumatic lifts, where the dogs can enjoy cheese licks as they get their ears and paws cleaned. With on-site veterinary care and classrooms, the National Training Center allows trainees—both human and canine—to be fully immersed in training and maximize learning as they hone their disaster-response readiness. The facility sets a new USAR training standard for the nation and perhaps the world, and continues to evolve to best serve its dogs.

When I approached Wilma with the idea of doing a book, the first thing she said was, "I don't want it about me." An understandable request, but being that she is the founder of the SDF, writing more than a sentence on the subject would require her involvement.

Still, besides her humble nature, there was a reason why she insisted on staying out of the spotlight: the SDF succeeded through the efforts of *many* special people. As such, I wrote the story from Wilma's perspective in order to highlight her importance in building the foundation, yet still keep the focus on these special dogs and people.

Much like the foundation itself, this narrative was built

not only from Wilma's experiences, but the experiences of SDF volunteers, dog trainers, firefighters, and search dog handlers, as well as from the consultation of books, newsletters, magazine articles, pictures, and videos pertaining to the events described. The reader saw the world through "Wilma's eyes," but the story was actually a conglomeration of all these SDF voices, interpreted via my words. In an effort to keep the reader at the forefront of the action, any situation Wilma was not present for was still told from her perspective, but was reconstructed based on the interviews of the person or persons physically involved in the event. A list of references I consulted for this book beyond my formal interviews is included in the back of the book.

Because this story began more than twenty years ago, memories are subject to fade. Many situations occurred under horrible stress and thus recollection can often be trying at best. I took small artistic liberties retelling certain events, but always made sure the story stayed as close to verified facts as possible. Certain sensitive information has been left out purposefully for privacy reasons. All quoted dialogue is based on formal interviews, and has been cross-referenced for accuracy whenever possible. In instances where memories or specific accounts differ, I have deferred to the person closest to the event. Any "thoughts" attributed to dogs were based on the opinions of the trainers or handlers at the time, and are merely my interpretations; I claim no special talents with animals nor veterinary training to shape these, only an active imagination. The dogs, well, their actions speak for themselves. I feel obliged to again remind the reader that this is a work of nonfiction, because what these dogs do often defies belief.

IN 2017, WILMA finally passed the benchmark of 168 teams trained, honoring her private commitment to the victims of the Oklahoma City bombing. Later that year, Wilma's final term on the SDF's advisory board came to a close. She is proud of what the SDF has accomplished, but to stay stagnant is to miss an opportunity for improvement. Retirement? Never. She has bigger things in mind.

Wilma still wears blue jeans, just like she used to when she would climb trees in her backyard with her canine companion Toffee (a story of whose loss, almost eighty years later, still brings tears to her eyes), because she stays working. Aside from her intermittent engagements as SDF founder—master of ceremonies for public events, donor engagements, and general council for the staff and trainers—independently, Wilma is busy creating another pilot program of training disaster search dogs from birth. She already has a litter of puppies in preparation homes. It won't be long before these puppies are hitting the obstacle course.

———

I LIKE TO think dogs' lives are so short because they love so intensely. The downside of this fact is that the only dog depicted in this story still living is the silver-screen-friendly Border Collie, Hunter, now almost three years retired, but still by Billy's side. All the others have passed away after happy retirements with their handlers, and usually a large contingent of firefighters by their sides. Since its start in 1996, the number of dogs saved or employed by the SDF has grown exponentially as well. As this book goes to print in 2019, the SDF has trained 210 search dogs and continues to add to the number every few months. The impact of these dogs is undeniable. To a person, every single individual I interviewed—from volunteer to trainer to handler—recalled, with the same affection as a parent recalling a child's first steps, a special dog that somehow touched their hearts. And that's exactly what these once-misfit dogs became to anyone who encountered them: family.

The feats of anyone involved with the SDF extend well beyond what can be contained in this book. As I was told many times during my course of research, the importance is not around the actions of the individual but the group as a whole. If a specific event or individual is not mentioned, it should not diminish their contributions to the foundation or Wilma's life. Any flaws or shortcomings in the writing or storytelling of this book (of which there are probably many) are mine alone. Any triumphs belong solely to Wilma, the SDF, their associates, and, of course, the dogs.

FOR THE NEXT generation of canine USAR teams, the work continues. A current roster of sixty-seven SDF dog teams is still short of what an expanding America and world needs. The dogs have deployed 168 times. Recently, in January 2018, it was close to home—a little too close. The Thomas Fire that scorched much of Southern California, tore through the Santa Paula hills, destroying a large portion of the SDF's new training facilities and forcing the evacuation of both dogs and people. Wilma saw her quiet airport home turned into a command center for California Fire and Emergency Services, with helicopters buzzing in and out around the clock. The subsequent winter rains turned the barren hillsides around the area into mudslides. Eighteen SDF teams were deployed to clear search areas. Eventually, the slides were cleared and cleaned up, and the SDF returned to rebuild.

The USAR job itself has not gotten any easier. Every deployment, the teams are still very much searching for a miracle. Though it is difficult to determine an exact number, since the live finds of 2010, combined human and canine USAR efforts have yielded live rescues only in the single digits. In Wilma's mind, this is a number that has to change. And so comes the purpose for the new litter of puppies, and perhaps the future direction of the SDF.

Although not much can be done about the lethality of certain disasters, the general consensus is that if a rescue team was able to get on a rubble pile faster—within a matter of hours—the probability of locating a live victim would increase substantially. Wilma's new vision involves a tiny private force, six individuals and two dogs, that would act almost as a 9-1-1 service for disaster searches. Teams would be always prepped and on-call, and in the air before the proverbial dust had settled. Removing FEMA from the equation, at least for the initial response, would require private aircraft and transportation to the disaster site, as well as locally sourced rescue assets, all of which would need to be pre-coordinated with the dog teams.

Taken together, the money and logistics needed to meet these requirements represent a tremendous obstacle. Some would say near insurmountable. Wilma has heard that before; though she admits to probably not seeing its completion within her lifetime, Wilma is never one to be counted out. She approaches it like she does every task— one persistent foot after the other.

For now, Wilma's time is consumed with prepping more of these special pups. Dog training in general— especially for puppies—requires full attention on the present, the silver lining of which is that there is no time for doubts about her new project to slink in. If training rescue dogs has taught Wilma one thing, it's that there is always hope. And that when you have the right dogs, nothing is impossible.

—*Paul Lobo*

You can join the Search Dog Foundation in helping transform rescued dogs into rescuers!

Learn more at: www.SearchDogFoundation.org.

ACKNOWLEDGMENTS

Thank you to my family. To my wife, Rebecca, who sacrificed a lot in order to let me wade into the murky (and often treacherous) waters of authorhood. She was my muse, my constructive critic, and my greatest supporter—always and forever. My son, Michael, aka "Iron Mike," too young to talk but the story in his eyes was inspiration enough. And to the rest of my family and friends, especially the ones that read my (terrible) rough drafts and still pushed me onward with a smile.

Thank you to Wilma for opening up about her life and trusting me with its amazing story. Her character is one-of-a-kind, and it influenced me throughout the writing process. Be it dogs or humans, what one can learn from this woman is without limits.

Thank you to Celeste Matesevac for giving an untested author a chance to write for the SDF. Had it not been for her kindness and encouragement, I doubt this manuscript would have made it past page 1. I can't wait to deliver this book to her amazing bookstore—BookEnds in Ojai, California.

Thank you to Pluis Davern and her family for sharing their wisdom and passion for training dogs. Our conversations were always hilarious and heartwarming, and I look forward to our next one—Chardonnay is on me, of course!

Thank you to George Haines, Debra Tosch, and the entire SDF staff. They welcomed my research missions with open arms and went out of their way to accommodate my requests for information. Time is not a luxury they can afford, yet they gave so much without complaint. I am forever indebted to such a wonderful organization. A special thank you also to SDF volunteer Karyn Newbill, whose wonderful photography graces the SDF campus and is showcased in this book.

Thank you to Rick Lee, Randy Gross, and Rob Cima for sharing their personal and often harrowing experiences as firefighters and search dog handlers. In a time when few would, they raised their hands to be sent. Courage like theirs is rare. I plan to tell my son their stories.

Thank you to Mike Antonucci. His passion for saving lives and dedication to service of our nation showed through in every word he spoke and contributed greatly to the book.

Thank you to Jim Boggeri, Andi Sutcliffe, Billy Monahan, and the others who shared their experiences as handlers—each one amazing and special. Their deeds and dogs touched so many in such a positive way, it was an honor to tell their tales.

Thank you to the greatest agent on the planet, Elizabeth Winick Rubinstein, and her staff at McIntosh & Otis. Liz always gave me a guiding hand and never let me doubt the book's potential. Confidence like that is contagious and it made the writing part easy.

Thank you to my editors, Marc Resnick and Hannah O'Grady, as well as the entire team at St. Martin's Press. Their efforts transformed this simple manuscript into something truly special.

I could go on for pages, but will conclude by thanking everyone who contributed energy along the way. Perhaps too many to mention, but trust me, you are not forgotten. This work belongs to you, too. You are, after all, part of the pack now.

REFERENCES

Ashley, S. (October 9, 2001). "When the Twin Towers Fell: one month after the attack on the World Trade Center, M.I.T. structural engineers offer their take on how and why the towers came down." *Scientific American*. Retrieved October 22, 2017, from www.scientificamerican.com

Bauer, N. K. (2011). *Dog Heroes of September 11th: a Tribute to America's Search and Rescue Dogs*. Freehold, NJ: Kennel Club Books.

Branson-Potts, H. (April 19, 2015). After Oklahoma City bombing, McVeigh's arrest almost went unnoticed. *Los Angeles Times*. Retrieved January 15, 2017, from www.latimes.com

Bulanda, S., & Bulanda, L. (2014). *Ready!:Training the Search and Rescue Dog*. Irvine, CA: I-5 Publishing.

Burnett, P. (2003). *Avalanche! Hasty Search: the Care and Training of Avalanche Search and Rescue Dogs*. Phoenix, AZ: Doral Pub.

Charleson, S. (2010). *Scent of the Missing: Love and Partnership with a Search-and-Rescue Dog*. Boston: Houghton Mifflin Harcourt.

Charleson, S. (2014). *The Possibility Dogs: What a Handful of "Unadoptables" Taught Me About Service, Hope, and Healing*. Boston: Mariner Books, Houghton Mifflin Harcourt.

Club, A. K. (n.d.). "Golden Retriever History & Training /Temperament." Retrieved January 10, 2017, from http://www.akc.org/dog-breeds/golden-retriever /detail/

DesRoches, Comerio, Eberhard, & Mooney. (2011). "Overview of the 2010 Haiti Earthquake" (Vol. 27, Ser. 1, pp. S1-S21, Rep.). Earthquake Engineering Research Institute. doi:10.1193/1.3630129.

Frankel, R. (2015). *War Dogs Tales of Canine Heroism, History, and Love*. NY: St. Martin's Griffin.

Gorman, J. (August 29, 2016). "With Dogs, It's What You Say—and How You Say It." *The New York Times*. Retrieved July 31, 2017, from www.nytimes.com

Hekman, J., DVM. (September 1, 2016). Helping Dogs Heal. "The Bark," *Fall 2016*(87), 43–49.

Hingson, M., & Flory, S. (2011). *Thunder Dog: The True*

Story of a Blind Man, His Guide Dog, and the Triumph of Trust. Nashville: Thomas Nelson.

Hoffman, J. (October 10, 2016). "Learning from Dogs as They Sniff Out Their World." *The New York Times.* Retrieved July 31, 2017, from www.nytimes.com

Hoffman, J. (July 31, 2017). "Is This Dog Dangerous? Shelters Struggle with Live-or-Die Tests." *The New York Times.* Retrieved July 31, 2017, from www.nytimes .com

Hoffman, J. (January 7, 2017). "To Rate How Smart Dogs Are, Humans Learn New Tricks." *The New York Times.* Retrieved July 31, 2017, from www.nytimes.com

Horowitz, A. (2017). *Being a Dog: Following the Dog into a World of Smell.* New York: Scribner.

Horowitz, A. (2017). *Inside of a Dog: What Dogs See, Smell, and Know.* New York: Simon & Schuster.

Independent Review of the U.S. Government Response to the Haiti Earthquake (Rep.). (2011).

Krakauer, J. (2010). *Where Men Win Glory: The Odyssey of Pat Tillman.* London: Atlantic.

McCormick, L. W. (n.d.). "Rescued Dog Finds New Job Rescuing People." *Dogs for Kids.*

Minutes of the California SAR Dog Confederation Meeting. (November 11, 1995).

Mone, G., & Brown, D. J. (2015). *The Boys in the Boat: The True Story of an American Team's Epic Journey to Win Gold at the 1936 Olympics.* New York: Viking.

Newmanjan, A. (January 20, 2016). "Animal Deaths

Down and Adoptions Up Amid Reforms at New York Shelters." *The New York Times*. Retrieved July 31, 2017, from www.nytimes.com

Otterman, S. (November 29, 2017). "Battered and Scarred, 'Sphere' Returns to 9/11 Site." *The New York Times*. Retrieved November 29, 2017, from www.nytimes .com

Pet Statistics. (n.d.). Retrieved November 28, 2017, from http://www.aspca.org/animal-homelessness/shelter -intake-and-surrender/pet-statistics

Ritland, M., & Brozek, G. (2015). *Team Dog: How to Train Your Dog—the Navy SEAL Way*. New York: G. P. Putnam's Sons.

Ritland, M., & Brozek, G. (2015). *Trident K9 Warriors: My Tales from the Training Ground to the Battlefield with Elite Navy SEAL Canines*. New York: St. Martin's Paperbacks.

Shelter Animals Count. (n.d.). Retrieved March 15, 2017, from http://shelteranimalscount.org/data/Explore-the -Data

U.S. Military Working Dog Training Handbook. (2013). Guilford, CT: Lyons Press.

Urban Search & Rescue Participants. (n.d.). Retrieved November 28, 2017, from http://www.fema.gov/urban -search-rescue-participants

Various. (2001–2017). *The Quest: Annual Report of the Search Dog Foundation*.

Various. (1997–2017). *The Bark Alert: Search Dog Foundation Newsletter.*

Various. (2004). *The 9/11 Commission Report* (Rep.).

Various. (2006). *The Federal Response to Hurricane Katrina Lessons Learned* (Rep.).

Various. (2015). *The Oklahoma City Bombing 20 Years Later* (Rep.). Retrieved December 12, 2016, from Federal Bureau of Investigation website: www.fbi.gov

Victor, D. (June 7, 2016). "Mourning Bretagne, a Search Dog and Symbol of 9/11 Heroism." *The New York Times.* Retrieved July 31, 2017, from www.nytimes .com